Care in Sport Coachi

GW00835847

While it is accepted that sport coaches should safeguard participants, *Care in Sport Coaching: Pedagogical Cases* argues that coaches have a duty of care that moves beyond protection and involves the development of caring relationships with athletes. Recent high-profile incidents of abuse in sport highlight the need to reposition coaching as a caring activity and to embed care within coach education and coaching policy.

Based around extended case studies, this book provides grounded accounts of how coaches care in their everyday practice. These case studies are analysed using multidisciplinary theoretical perspectives to illustrate and problematise how coaches care. Conclusions are provided, based on these analyses, that will help coach educators, researchers and policy makers establish care as a key facet of everyday sport coaching activities. Additionally, the book offers guidelines that will aid practitioners to enact care in their practice.

This is important reading for coaches, researchers, lecturers and students who are concerned with the role of coaches and the development of coaching practice.

Colum Cronin is Senior Lecturer in Physical Education and Sport Coaching at Liverpool John Moores University, UK. Colum's research concerns youth sport coaching, coach education and coaching in community contexts. Colum's doctorate, which is the genesis of this book, focused on the lives of sport coaches. He has supported national governing bodies of sport to evaluate their coaching and has experience in both youth and adult basketball coaching in the UK. Indeed, as a practitioner, he has experience coaching in the voluntary, public and private sectors, whilst working as a coach educator.

Kathleen Armour is Pro-Vice Chancellor (education) at the University of Birmingham, UK; Fellow of the Academy of Social Sciences; and International Fellow of the National Academy of Kinesiology. Kathleen's research focuses on career-long professional development for physical education teachers and sport coaches, and she is particularly interested in bridging the gaps between theory/research and practice. Kathleen has received over £2.5 million of research funding from research councils, charities and industries. In her most recent books, Kathleen has developed a new translational mechanism – 'pedagogical cases' – to support practitioner learning and influence research agendas.

Routledge Research in Sports Coaching

The *Routledge Research in Sports Coaching* series provides a platform for leading experts and emerging academics in this important discipline to present ground-breaking work on the history, theory, practice and contemporary issues of sports coaching. The series sets a new benchmark for research in sports coaching, and offers a valuable contribution to the wider sphere of sports studies.

Available in this series:

Sport Coaching Research and Practice
Ontology, Interdisciplinarity and Critical Realism
Julian North

Leadership in Sports Coaching
A Social Identity Approach
Paul Cummins, Ian O'Boyle and Tony Cassidy

Learning to Mentor in Sports Coaching
A Design Thinking Approach
Edited by Fiona C. Chambers

Care in Sport Coaching
Pedagogical Cases
Edited by Colum Cronin and Kathleen Armour

For a full list of available titles please visit: www.routledge.com.

Care in Sport Coaching

Pedagogical Cases

**Edited by Colum Cronin
and Kathleen Armour**

Routledge
Taylor & Francis Group

LONDON AND NEW YORK

First published 2019 by Routledge

2 Park Square, Milton Park, Abingdon, Oxfordshire OX14 4RN

52 Vanderbilt Avenue, New York, NY 10017

Routledge is an imprint of the Taylor & Francis Group, an informa business

First issued in paperback 2019

British Library Cataloguing-in-Publication Data
A catalogue record for this book is available from the British Library

Library of Congress Cataloging-in-Publication Data
A catalog record for this book has been requested

ISBN: 978-0-8153-6349-1 (hbk)
ISBN: 978-0-367-89627-0 (pbk)

Typeset in Times New Roman
by Apex CoVantage, LLC

Colum Cronin: To Erin and Jacob, and all the family and friends that 'care for' them.

Kathleen Armour: To Charlie, Georgie and Jamie. Still great 'kids.'

Contents

List of contributors   ix
Acknowledgements   xi

1   **Introduction to care in coaching**   1
    COLUM CRONIN AND KATHLEEN ARMOUR

2   **Care theory and sport coaching**   15
    COLUM CRONIN, KATHLEEN ARMOUR
    AND LORI GANO-OVERWAY

3   **Why pedagogical case studies?**   30
    KATHLEEN ARMOUR AND COLUM CRONIN

4   **Nurturing care in sport coaching: Jane's story**   44
    COLUM CRONIN AND KATHLEEN ARMOUR

5   **Caring through science and autonomy: Terry's story**   62
    COLUM CRONIN, KATHLEEN ARMOUR AND KEVIN ENRIGHT

6   **Caring for, and with, others: Julie's story**   82
    COLUM CRONIN, SIMON ROBERTS, OWEN CRONIN
    AND KATHLEEN ARMOUR

7   **The cost of caring: Dave's story**   101
    COLUM CRONIN, JOHN HAYTON, SÖREN HJÄLM
    AND KATHLEEN ARMOUR

8   Conclusions, guidelines and future questions   124
    COLUM CRONIN AND KATHLEEN ARMOUR

    Index   136

Contributors

Dr Owen Cronin is Rheumatologist and General Physician in the Rheumatic Diseases Unit, Western General Hospital, Edinburgh. He has provided medical care for amateur, semi-professional and professional athletes in football and athletics among other sports in Cork City, Ireland.

Dr Kevin Enright is Senior Lecturer in Sports Coaching and Coaching Science at Liverpool John Moores University. Previously, Kevin worked as a Strength and Conditioning Coach supporting a range of athletes who were preparing for Olympic and Commonwealth Games, Premier League footballers and international football teams. Kevin's research interests include understanding how training periodisation can influence muscle adaptations that alter injury risk in athletic populations.

Dr Lori Gano-Overway is Associate Professor and Coaching Programme Coordinator at Bridgewater College. She has worked in coaching education for over 20 years across a variety of contexts. As an Association for Applied Sport Psychology certified mental performance consultant, she also collaborates with coaches on creating environments to cultivate positive athletic experiences.

Dr John Hayton is Senior Lecturer in Sport Development at Liverpool John Moores University. His research uses social theory to examine the delivery of sport and physical recreation in and by the non-profit and voluntary sector. Specific areas of John's research have centred upon volunteer management and volunteering development across a range of sporting contexts.

Dr Sören Hjälm is Senior Lecturer in the School of Health Sciences at Örebro University, Sweden. His research and teaching is focused on leadership and burnout among soccer coaches. He is a certified cognitive behavioural therapist and regularly works with athletes and coaches, helping them to manage stress in their career.

Dr Simon Roberts is Reader in Sport and Exercise Pedagogy at Liverpool John Moores University. Previous publications and research interests include the complexities of the talent identification and development processes in youth football, and relative age inequalities in both youth and elite sport.

Acknowledgements

Our thanks go to the coaches whose experiences are described in the case studies. Not only do these coaches endeavour to care for their athletes but also they willingly shared their time and expertise so that others may benefit.

1 Introduction to care in coaching

Colum Cronin and Kathleen Armour

Righteous indignation is often dismissed or ridiculed as 'ranting' or 'virtue signalling.' Nevertheless, when it comes to sport coaching, perhaps we should be indignantly righteous more often. Across the globe abysmal incidents in have, and continue to occur in sport coaching. High-profile examples of unethical coach behaviour include sexual abuse in soccer (UK), drug abuse in young football players (Australia), academic and financial fraud in basketball (US), and physical abuse and overtraining in diving (China). These have all been enacted by coaches. In most cases, coaches at the centre of such scandals have been educated formally by coach educators and are under the auspices of official sports governing bodies. In such instances, the absence of care (and protection) for the holistic athlete is an alarming yet common theme (Gearity, 2012). There is evidence that such incidents are not isolated, nor culturally exclusive (Lang & Harthill, 2015). Thus, when it comes to the topic of care in sport coaching, some righteous indignation is justified. It will, however, take more than righteous indignation to improve the caring practice of coaches. Rather, it is contended here that coaching needs to be repositioned as an activity with caring at its very core. As such, coaches need to have access to resources that explain, illustrate and analyse *how* coaches care for athletes in sporting contexts, prompting them to reflect on their own practices. This book aims to be such a resource. Unfortunately, the book is clearly needed.

Although there are far too many reported – and unreported – examples of uncaring and abusive coaching practice, it is also important to remember that many (most) coaches care passionately about sport and care deeply for athletes. Of course, these caring coaches receive less media attention than those who are abusive or uncaring, but they do their best for athletes often at great personal cost. Many coaches invest labour and financial resources to support athletes (Knust & Fisher, 2015). Coaches, both paid and unpaid, take time to nurture athletes' wider social skills and prepare them for life's challenges (Knust & Fisher, 2015; Fisher, Bejar, Larsen, Fynes, & Gearity, 2017).When life events challenge athletes, they often turn to their coach for trusted and supportive counsel (Fisher et al., 2017). In other words, when coaching is done well, it is a caring activity where coaches encourage people in ways that help them to flourish as athletes and as people. The media rarely documents these instances. Thus, it is that coaching as a profession can be described as having a paradoxical care crisis. The crisis is characterised by the simultaneous presence of abusive, uncaring coaching practice and the unheralded, often-unseen caring practice that is at the core of a coach's duty to care.

In the UK, the premise that coaches have a duty of care is widely accepted by national governing bodies (Rhind, McDermott, Lambert, & Koleva, 2014). This is partly because coaching has long been associated with teaching (Jones, 2009), which has a similar duty of care. Both teachers and coaches are powerful individuals who aim to impart and construct knowledge through their pedagogies. Historical accounts of coaching in the UK have also noted strong links between coaching and teaching (e.g. Day & Carpenter, 2016), dating back to the Victorian era when teachers performed the roles of coaches in public schools[1] (Holt, 1989; Light, 2010). Today, much coaching continues to occur in schools and the lines between teaching and coaching can become blurred. For example, in 2011 in the UK, 19% of coaching occurred in schools and in single sports clubs (36%) that typically had close links to educational institutions – e.g., shared use of facilities or community coaching programmes (Sports Coach UK, 2011).

The links between teaching and coaching have been further reinforced by researchers (e.g. Armour, 2011) who have recognised the commonalities between teaching and coaching through the term, 'sport pedagogy.' Sport pedagogy is a concept that is contested, but is generally accepted as a subdiscipline of kinesiology (Tinning, 2008),[2] and concentrates on the synthesis of multidisciplinary knowledge to address the sport and physical activity needs of learners (Armour & Chambers, 2014). This conception of sport pedagogy largely eschews divisions between coaching, physical education (PE) and other areas of physical activity by placing an emphasis on the primacy of learning through a pedagogical relationship (Armour, 2014; 2011). Consistent with this notion of sport pedagogy, a large corpus of coach behaviour literature has emphasised actions that are common to both teachers in the classroom and coaches on the field of play, such as providing instructions and questioning (Cope, Partington, & Harvey, 2017; Tharp & Gallimore, 1976; Gallimore & Tharp, 2004). Thus, from a sport pedagogy perspective, teaching and coaching share similar behaviours and a similar focus on the needs of learners. Recognising the commonalities between coaching and teaching within the discipline of sport pedagogy is important because it establishes the notion that coaches have a duty of care akin to teachers.

To greater and lesser extents, 'a duty of care' is often accepted as an uncontroversial concept by governing bodies, coach educators and coaches themselves (Garratt, Piper, & Taylor, 2013). Primarily, an understanding of this duty of care is largely concerned with non-malevolence – i.e., not harming participants. In practice, however, it has been suggested that a duty of care has been 'taken for granted' in coaching (Cronin & Armour, 2017), or that it has morphed into protecting coaches themselves (Garratt et al., 2013). For example, Harthill and Lang (2014) demonstrate that for governing bodies, child protection, safeguarding and duty of care are areas that compete for resources against other agendas such as anti-doping and equity. The sample for this research consisted of staff at national governing bodies in the UK and the findings suggested that, in practice, senior managers have very little interest in the concepts of child protection and duty of care. Indeed, Harthill and Lang (2014) lament that some senior managers continue to focus more on protecting their own exposure to litigation than developing a genuine interest in social justice and protecting the human rights of sport participants.

Child protection, safeguarding and duty of care are the minimum standards we should expect of coaches and all those involved in sport. Institutional bodies have been established to ensure these standards are implemented including the UK's Child Protection in Sport Unit and the United States Centre for Safe Sport. Similarly, safeguarding procedures such as criminal background checks, and safeguarding policies in national governing bodies, clubs and schools have also been developed over the past 30 years to ensure minimum standards of safeguarding are implemented (Brackenridge & Rhind, 2014). Internationally, support has also been provided by organisations such as the United

Nations Office on Sport for Development and Peace, and UNICEF (Brackenridge, Fasting, Kirby, & Leahy, 2010; Reynard, 2013). Yet, despite this work, Brackenridge and Rhind (2014) suggest that similar to the governing body staff reported in the research by Harthill and Lang (2014), coaches continue to focus on what humans do (i.e. sport performance) rather than humans themselves. Thus, work on child protection, safeguarding, and 'duty of care' has yet to transform the sporting habitus to one where child protection and 'duty of care' are considered 'meaningful rather than superficial' concepts (Harthill & Lang, 2014, p. 622).

Care as a concept builds upon the important ethic of non-malevolence inherent in extant child protection courses and policies. Theoretically, care is in keeping with Harthill and Lang's (2014) call for a 'meaningful' practice, and Brackenridge and Rhind's (2014, p. 334) ideal of a 'humanitarian shift in sport.' More specifically, care is concerned with building affective, reciprocal and dialogical relationships that serve the needs of others (Noddings, 2013). Care is therefore, a complex concept, which seeks to do more than 'not harm' another individual. It is a relational and dynamic construct that envelops safeguarding, but also includes serving the beneficence of athletes, and respecting their human rights (Cronin, Walsh, Quayle, Whittaker, & Whitehead, 2018). In simple terms, care involves not harming athletes, but also involves listening to, being concerned about, being focused on, and where appropriate meeting their needs (Jones, 2009). With a few exceptions however (see Chapter 2 for these), care is rarely discussed in coaching literature. Consequently, how coaches care for athletes has not been problematised (Cronin & Armour, 2017). Indeed, to some extent, a line has been drawn prematurely under the theorisation of care in coaching. This may be due to the association of 'duty of care' with formal organisational and legal child protection policies. The under-theorisation of care as a coaching concept is apparent in the absence of any academic textbook that focuses on the practice of care in coaching. This is remiss because it means that coaching researchers have not extensively analysed *how* coaches enact care, in what circumstances, and for whom. As a result, we do not have adequate accounts of how coaches move beyond minimum safety procedures and non-malevolence, to build caring relationships that respect and benefit athletes as both humans and performers (Brackenridge & Rhind, 2014).

To summarise thus far, practicing coaches, coach educators and employers such as national governing bodies have a widely accepted duty of care. At the same time, the wider media has with some justification, promulgated a moral panic about care in coaching. In that context, it is surprising that coaches, coach educators and national governing bodies have generated little academic analysis of *how* they should enact care. This book seeks to address this gap. It seeks to move beyond the righteous indignation that accompanies appalling instances of careless and abusive coaching. It suggests we move beyond the important minimum standard of child protection towards a gold standard of caring relationships. It seeks to inform debate so that we can move beyond a superficial acknowledgment of a coach's duty of care, and provide a critical problematisation of *how* coaches can meaningfully care. To that end, this chapter proceeds by positioning coaching as an interpersonal and situated activity. This is important, because it establishes that how coaches enact care will always be contextualised by their pedagogical setting and by whom they coach. Finally, the chapter concludes by outlining the remainder of the book, which is organised around, contextualised, pedagogical cases and multidisciplinary analyses to interrogate and illustrate how coaches can enact care in their own sporting world.

Caring in the context of sport coaching

Research in coaching has advocated that to be a coach is to be part of an interdependent relationship with athletes (Cronin & Armour, 2017). Both psychological and sociological literature has illustrated this point. For example, Jowett (2012, p. 1) has declared that "successful coaching, or performance success more specifically, is the combined inter-relation between the coach and the athlete." This conclusion is based upon her work with colleagues, which has problematised coach–athlete relationships through the 3C+1 coach–athlete relationship model (Jowett, 2007; Jowett & Cockerill, 2003; Jowett & Meek, 2000; Jowett, 2012). The model, which is developed from a psychological perspective, stresses that coaching involves being complementary to athletes' needs, being committed to athletes, and being 'close' with athletes. Since, its development, the 3C+1 model has been applied in a variety of coaching contexts, and is one of the most highly cited concepts in sport coaching research (Rangeon, Gilbert &

Bruner, 2012). In addition to Jowett's work, other authors writing from a psychological perspective (e.g. Côté & Gilbert, 2009) have also clarified that coaching is an interpersonal act between a coach and an athlete, with the aim of helping the athlete to flourish. Thus, it is appropriate that this book on care in coaching is concerned with the interdependent relationship between coaches and athletes. After all, without an athlete, you cannot be a caring sport coach.

In conceiving of coaching as an interpersonal relationship, this book also recognises that coaching is a dynamic and complex activity. The premise for this position is that both coaches and athletes are complex because of their ever-changing biographies, personalities, motives and skills. This explains why research has established that coaching is a relational activity, but has found it difficult to understanding the complex and dynamic nature of coach–athlete relationships (Jones, 2012). Not deterred, however, sociologically informed coaching research has sought to make sense of the complexity of coach and athlete relationships. For example, a body of literature has explored power in coaching by using the work of French social theorist, Foucault (e.g. Denison, 2007; Denison & Mills, 2014; Lang, 2010; Taylor & Garratt, 2010). This literature and that of Purdy, Potrac and Jones (2008) has shown that coaches are often in positions of authority, can be held in high esteem by athletes and their role involves monitoring and supporting the progress of athletes. With this in mind, it is clear that coaches are powerful individuals in the lives of athletes because they have gatekeeping influences over athletes' bodies, sporting opportunities and career prospects. Paradoxically, this means that coaches are both well placed to care for athletes, or conversely to enact harm. On this theme, Raakman, Dorsch and Rhind (2010) identified a typology of abusive behaviours where coaches misuse their power to enact harm through physical abuse, psychological abuse, sexual abuse and neglect. In terms of the scale of this harm, a study in the UK involving 6,000 young people reported that 12% of participants experienced regular emotional abuse linked to unhelpful and disproportionate criticism from coaches. Twenty-one percent of the young people in the report experienced sexual harassment involving coaches, and yet the report also highlights that the majority of young people had positive experience of coaches and sport (Stafford, Alexander, & Fry, 2013). Indeed, this paradox of harm and beneficence is also apparent in an International

Olympic Committee consensus statement which stresses the "need for research exploring the efficacy and effectiveness of specific strategies that can protect *and* (author's emphasis) promote the well-being of youth athletes" (Bergeron et al., 2015). The emphasis on both the protection and beneficence of athletes once again demonstrates the coaches' power laden role. Of course, this power laden role uniquely positions coaches to care for athletes in sporting contexts.

Notwithstanding the influential position that coaches as carers hold, coaches themselves, are subject to powerful stimuli within coach–athlete relationships. This is because power is not mono-directional. For example, an athlete may withdraw their effort and this can be a concern for coaches whose career depends on the sporting performance of athletes (Purdy, Jones & Cassidy, 2009). In addition, parents, clubs and national governing bodies may monitor coaching practices (Lang, 2010). This can be a concern for coaches because the tenure of their relationship with athletes can be linked to funding that is provided by these parents, clubs or sporting bodies. Thus, coaches' actions should not be viewed in isolation but in the context of a wider social network that has economic and political power.

To explain how coaching actions, such as a coaches' approach to caring, are influenced by the dispositions, norms and rules within clubs and national governing bodies, coaching researchers have drawn on the work of Bourdieu (Cushion & Jones, 2012; Light & Evans, 2013; Purdy et al., 2009). This work has provided rich accounts of coaching in environments such as professional football, rugby and rowing. For instance, in a critical account of coaching philosophy, Cushion and Partington (2014) illustrate how the philosophies that coaches profess are often in accordance with the accepted norms of others within their club rather than authentic personal accounts of their own values and beliefs. This is because representing the accepted practice within a given social context can be key to maintaining a coach's position or status. Extrapolating from this an understanding of how coaches care in a context may be influenced by the prevailing practices or a desire to maintain or extend their status within this context. On this theme, authors have drawn upon Erving Goffman's dramaturgical metaphor to compare coaches to actors who deliver a performance in response to the needs of a given audience – e.g., athletes, parents, administrators (Jones, Potrac, Cushion, Ronglan & Davey, 2011).

Once more on this theme, researchers have also utilised Howard Garfinkel's ethnomethods to illustrate how coaches' actions may be reflective of the wider social structures they inhabit (Miller & Cronin, 2013; Jones & Corsby, 2015; Evans, 2017). Coaches, therefore, have the difficult task of orchestrating sporting performances in ever-changing environments that include a variety of stakeholders (parents, fellow staff, administrators and supporters). Accordingly, Cushion and Partington (2014, p. 13) conclude that researchers should not "under recognise the influence of social structure upon coaches' beliefs, actions and discourses." Thus, as we move forward to consider care in coaching, we must acknowledge that care will not only occur within power laden relationships between a coach and athlete but also that these relationships are situated and influenced by a set of actors and wider social, economic and political conditions. Undoubtedly, these wider social influences and the wider network of actors that coaches encounter will influence what coaches care about and how coaches care.

Organisation of this book

This chapter began by acknowledging some of the abusive incidents associated with sport coaching. These incidents occur across a range of cultures and international environments. For example, an uncaring 'culture of fear' has been highlighted in high performance British cycling (British Cycling and UK Sport, 2017). To address these concerns, researchers have called for a transformative approach to sport which is more human focused and which prioritises the human experience over sport performance (Brackenridge & Rhind, 2014; Harthill & Lang, 2014). Such an approach is consistent with existing relational notions of care. Specifically, Noddings' (2013, p. 2) care ethic argues that carers need to be "receptive, related and responsive" to the needs of others. She argues that pedagogical relationships should always involve care, and she characterises care as dialogue, empathy, respect and concern for others. As an interpersonal relationship, Noddings also sees care as complex and acknowledges that what will be considered caring for one person could be inadequate or demeaning to another. Thus, caring is a relational and dynamic activity that eschews universal rules. Noddings' (2013, p. 11) summarises this point well by stating:

How we care depends not upon rules or at least not wholly upon rules – not on a prior determination of what is fair or equitable – but upon a constellation of conditions that is viewed through both the eyes of the one-caring and the eyes of the cared for.

With Armour's (2011) notion of sport pedagogy in mind, it appears that Noddings' sentiments are relevant to coaching. For example, similar to understandings of the coach–athlete relationship (Jowett, 2007), Noddings' care theory is relational in that it always involves both a carer and coach. Additionally, Noddings view of care as dynamic and complex is consistent with sociological understandings of the coaching process (e.g., Evans, 2017). Accordingly, this book proceeds by further explaining and analysing Noddings' care theory in Chapter 2. Chapter 2 also considers how Noddings' care ethic has been used in extant coaching research, while also critically considering the limitations of Noddings' work. This is important because Noddings' emphasis on building caring relationships has potential to inform the transformative human focused approach to sport called for by researchers (e.g. Brackenridge & Rhind, 2014) and to be enacted by coaches.

Following on from Chapter 2, the remainder of the book is structured around four pedagogical case studies (Chapter 4–7). These case studies of coaches were derived using methods outlined in Chapter 3. Indeed, Chapter 3 provides an explanation of how these cases were constructed as part of a larger research project, which helps readers when considering the authenticity of cases in Chapters 4–7. Contextually rich descriptions of coaches have been constructed because as outlined care involves more than universal rules (Noddings, 2013), and coaching is a dynamic situated activity (Miller & Cronin, 2013). Thus, how we care in one context – e.g., on the field of play – might be different to how we care in another, for example, on transport, in hotels, in therefore, situated and relevant pedagogical cases can be a useful resource that prompt coaches to consider their own practice and to effect change in their worlds (Armour, 2014). To that end then, the four case studies illustrate, analyse and problematise how coaches care in practice (Chapters 4–7). The structure of each caring case study chapter follows a similar format: a narrative of a coach is presented including biographical information and critical incidents in their practice derived from data collected as part of a larger research project. Following the presentation of each caring case, multidisciplinary analyses are provided. These perspectives offer theoretically informed analyses from a wide range of disciplinary perspectives including pedagogy, psychology, sociology and sport medicine. Links are also made between the care theory introduced in Chapter 2 and the grounded experiences of the coaches. These analyses thus provide unique insights into care from multiple perspectives and direct readers to further literature that may be relevant to their coaching worlds. Finally, the concluding chapter is reflective and focuses on identifying practical implications of the material presented. In doing so, the book makes three significant contributions:

1   It repositions coaching as a caring activity, reminding readers of the daunting complexity, challenge and humanity of coaching practice.
2   It prompts reflection on practice in new ways by linking different theoretical perspectives with grounded accounts of caring and coaching.
3   It provides evidence-based yet tentative guidelines for care that readers may find helpful to take back to their own coaching context.

Notes

1   Public schools in the Victorian era (1831–1901, named after the British queen of the day), were typically exclusive fee-paying schools who were independent of government – e.g., Eton. Upper class male youths typically attended these schools on a boarding basis. The schools often encouraged sport as a means of developing character and improving athleticism among pupils.
2   Kinesiology is as North American term associated with the study of human movement. In the UK, kinesiology is perhaps akin to sport and exercise sciences.

Bibliography

Armour, K. M. (2011). *Sport pedagogy: An introduction for teaching and coaching* (1st ed.). London: Routledge.
Armour, K. M. (2014). *Pedagogical cases in physical education and youth sport* (1st ed.). Oxon: Routledge.
Armour, K. M., & Chambers, F. C. (2014). 'Sport & Exercise Pedagogy': The case for a new integrative sub-discipline in the field of Sport &

Exercise Sciences/Kinesiology/Human Movement Sciences. *Sport, Education and Society*, *19*(7), 855–868. doi:10.1080/13573322.2013.8 59132

Bergeron, M. F., Mountjoy, M., Armstrong, N., Chia, M., Côté, J., Emery, C. A., . . . Engebretsen, L. (2015). International Olympic Committee consensus statement on youth athletic development. *British Journal of Sports Medicine*, *49*(13), 843–851. doi:10.1136/bjsports-2015-094962

Brackenridge, C. H., Fasting, K., Kirby, S., & Leahy, T. (2010). *Protecting children from violence in sport: A review with a focus on industrialized countries*. Florence: UNICEF.

Brackenridge, C. H., & Rhind, D. (2014). Child protection in sport: Reflections on thirty years of science and activism. *Social Sciences*, *3*(3), 326–340. doi:10.3390/socsci3030326

British Cycling and UK Sport. (2017). *Report of the independent panel into the climate and culture of the world class programme in British Cycling*. London: British Cycling and UK Sport.

Cope, E., Partington, M., & Harvey, S. (2017). A review of the use of a systematic observation method in coaching research between 1997 and 2016. *Journal of Sports Sciences*, *35*(20), 2042–2050. doi:10.1080/0264 0414.2016.1252463

Côté, J., & Gilbert, W. (2009). An integrative definition of coaching effectiveness and expertise. *International Journal of Sports Science & Coaching*, *4*(3), 307–323. doi:10.1260/174795409789623892

Cronin, C., & Armour, K. M. (2017). 'Being' in the coaching world: New insights on youth performance coaching from an interpretative phenomenological approach. *Sport, Education and Society*, *22*(8), 919–931. doi:10.108 0/13573322.2015.1108912

Cronin, C., Walsh, B., Quayle, L., Whittaker, E., & Whitehead, A. (2018). Carefully supporting autonomy: Learning coaching lessons and advancing theory from women's netball in England. *Sports Coaching Review*, 1–23. doi:10.1080/21640629.2018.1429113

Cushion, C., & Jones, R. L. (2012). A Bourdieusian analysis of cultural reproduction: Socialisation and the 'hidden curriculum' in professional football. *Sport, Education and Society*, *19*(3), 1–23. doi:10.1080/13573 322.2012.666966

Cushion, C., & Partington, M. (2014). A critical analysis of the conceptualisation of 'coaching philosophy'. *Sport, Education and Society*. doi:10.10 80/13573322.2014.958817

Day, D., & Carpenter, T. (2016). *A history of sport coaching in Britain: Overcoming amateurism* (1st ed.). London: Routledge.

Denison, J. (2007). Social theory for coaches: A Foucauldian reading of one athlete's poor performance. *International Journal of Sport Science and Coaching*, *2*(4), 369–384. doi:10.1260/174795407783359777

Denison, J., & Mills, J. P. (2014). Planning for distance running: Coaching with Foucault. *Sports Coaching Review, 3*(1), 1–16. doi:10.1080/216406 29.2014.953005

Evans, B. (2017). Sports coaching as action-in-context: Using ethnomethodological conversation analysis to understand the coaching process. *Qualitative Research in Sport, Exercise and Health, 9*(1), 111–132. doi:10.1080/2159676X.2016.1246473

Fisher, L. A., Bejar, M. P., Larsen, L. K., Fynes, J. M., & Gearity, B. T. (2017). Caring in U.S. National Collegiate Athletic Association division 1 sport: The Perspectives of 18 Female and Male Head Coaches. *International Journal of Sports Science and Coaching, 12*(1), 75–91. doi:10.1177/1747954116684388

Gallimore, R., & Tharp, R. (2004). What a coach can teach a teacher, 1975–2004: Reflections and reanalysis of John Wooden's teaching practices. *The Sport Psychologist, 18*(2), 119–137. doi:10.1123/tsp.18.2.119

Garratt, D., Piper, H., & Taylor, B. (2013). 'Safeguarding' sports coaching: Foucault, genealogy and critique. *Sport, Education and Society, 18*(5), 615–629. doi:10.1080/13573322.2012.736861

Gearity, B. (2012). Coach as unfair and uncaring. *Journal for the Study of Sports and Athletes in Education, 6*(2), 173–200. doi:10.1179/ssa.2012.6.2.173

Harthill, M., & Lang, M. (2014). 'I know people think I'm a complete pain in the neck': An examination of the introduction of child protection and 'safeguarding' in English sport from the perspective of national governing body safeguarding lead officers. *Social Sciences, 3*(4), 606–627. doi:10.3390/socsci3040606

Holt, R. (1989). *Sport and the British: A modern history.* Oxford: Clarendon Press.

Jones, R. L. (2009). Coaching as caring (the smiling gallery): Accessing hidden knowledge. *Physical Education and Sport Pedagogy, 14*(4), 377–390. doi:10.1080/17408980801976551

Jones, R. L. (2012). Editorial. *Sports Coaching Review, 1*(1), 1–3.

Jones, R. L., & Corsby, C. (2015). A case for coach Garfinkel: Decision making and what we already know. *Quest, 67*(4), 439–449. doi:10.1080/00336297.2015.1082919

Jones, R. L., Potrac, P., Cushion, C., Ronglan, L., & Davey, C. (2011). Erving Goffman: Interaction and impression management, playing the coaching role. In R. Jones, P. Potrac, C. Cushion, & L. Ronglan, *The sociology of sports coaching* (pp. 15–27). London: Routledge.

Jowett, S. (2007). Interdependence analysis and the 3 + 1 Cs in the coach-athlete relationship. In S. Jowett, D. Lavallee, S. Jowett, & D. Lavallee (Eds.), *Social psychology in sport* (pp. 15–27). Champaign, IL: Human Kinetics.

Jowett, S. (2012, Autumn). The coach-athlete relationship. *The Sport and Exercise Scientist*, 16–17.

Jowett, S., & Cockerill, I. M. (2003). Olympic medallists' perspective of the athlete. *Psychology of Sport and Exercise*, *4*(4), 313–331. doi:10.1016/S1469-0292(02)00011-0

Jowett, S., & Meek, G. A. (2000). The coach-athlete relationship in married couples: An exploratory content analysis. *The Sport Psychologist*, *14*(2), 157–175. doi:10.1123/tsp.14.2.157

Knust, S. K., & Fisher, L. A. (2015). NCAA division I female head coaches' experiences of exemplary care within coaching. *International Sport Coaching Journal*, *2*(2), 94–107. doi:10.1123/iscj.2013-0045

Lang, M. (2010). Surveillance and conformity in competitive youth swimming. *Sport, Education and Society*, *15*(1), 19–37. doi:10.1080/1357 3320903461152

Lang, M., & Harthill, M. (2015). *Safeguarding, child protection and abuse in sport: International perspectives in research, policy and practice.* London: Routledge.

Light, R. L. (2010). A 'strange . . . absurd . . . and somewhat injurious influence'? Cricket, professional coaching in the public schools and the 'gentleman amateur'. *Sport in History*, *30*(1), 8–31. doi:10.1080/17460261003616609

Light, R. L., & Evans, J. R. (2013). Dispositions of elite-level Australian rugby coaches towards game sense: Characteristics of their coaching habitus. *Sport, Education and Society*, *18*(3), 407–423. doi:10.1080/13573322.2011.593506

Miller, P. K., & Cronin, C. (2013). Rethinking the factuality of 'contextual' factors in an ethnomethodological mode: Towards a reflexive understanding of action-context dynamism in the theorization of coaching. *Sports Coaching Review*, *1*(2), 106–123. doi:10.1080/21640629.2013.790166

Noddings, N. (2013). *Caring: A relational approach to ethics and moral education* (2nd ed.). London: University of California Press.

Purdy, L., Potrac, P., & Jones, R. (2008). Power, consent and resistance: An autoethnography of competitive rowing. *Sport, education and society*, *13*(3), 319–336. doi: 10.1080/13573320802200693

Purdy, L., Jones, R. L., & Cassidy, T. (2009). Negotiation and capital: Athletes' use of power in an elite men's rowing program. *Sport, Education and Society*, *14*(3), 321–338. doi:10.1080/13573320903037796

Raakman, E., Dorsch, K., & Rhind, D. (2010). The development of a typology of abusive coaching behaviours within youth sport. *International Journal of Sports Science & Coaching*, *5*(4), 503–515. doi:10.1260/1747-9541.5.4.503

Rangeon, S., Gilbert, W., & Bruner, M. (2012). Mapping the world of coaching science: A citation network analysis. *Journal of Coaching Science: A Citation Network Analysis*, *5*(1), 83–108. doi:10.1123/jce.5.1.83

Reynard, S. (2013). *Child safeguarding at the 2013 beyond sport summit.* London: UNICEF.

Rhind, D., McDermott, J., Lambert, E., & Koleva, I. (2014). A review of safeguarding cases in sport. *Child Abuse Review, 24*(6), 418–426. doi:10.1002/car.2306

Sports Coach UK. (2011). *Sports coaching in the UK III.* Leeds: Sports Coach UK.

Stafford, A., Alexander, K., & Fry, D. (2013). *Playing through pain: Children and young people's experiences of physical aggression and violence in sport.* Edinburgh: University of Edinburgh/NSPCC Centre for UK-wider Learning in Child Protection.

Taylor, W. G., & Garratt, D. (2010). The professionalisation of sports coaching: Relations of power, resistance and compliance. *Sport Education and Society, 15*(1), 121–139. doi:10.1080/13573320903461103

Tharp, R. G., & Gallimore, R. (1976). Basketballs John Wooden: What a coach can teach a teacher. *Psychology Today, 9*(8), 74–78.

Tinning, R. (2008). Pedagogy, sport pedagogy, and the field of kinesiology. *Quest, 60*(3), 405–424. doi:10.1080/00336297.2008.10483589

2   Care theory and sport coaching

Colum Cronin, Kathleen Armour and Lori Gano-Overway

Despite being recognised as an essential aspect of coaching (Cronin & Armour, 2017), care has rarely been considered in coaching literature. An exception to this is Robyn Jones' (2009) ethnography 'The Smiling Gallery.' Although Jones primarily uses the paper to advocate for autoethnographic explorations of sport coaching, the narrative within Jones' article also raises the issue of care in youth coaching. More precisely, in the autoethnographic vignette, Jones describes an incident when he empathetically recognises a young nervous football (soccer) player at a trial event and provides a supportive smile to ease the young player's worries. This caring act prompts Jones to reminisce about his own experiences as a young athlete, and how he longed for a caring coach. In doing so, Jones was able to provide a personal and insightful account of care from both sides of the coach–athlete relationship.

More recently, Annerstedt and Eva-Carin (2014) have provided a case study of a now retired adult high-performance coach. Through their case study, the authors depict a caring coach who listens to players, empathises with the challenges athletes face, and supports players through times of conflict. The authors reinforce Jones' (2009) notion that caring acts may be a part of coach–athlete relationships, and they also illustrate that care is not confined to youth sport coaching. In addition to these accounts, Carwyn Jones (2015) provides an account from the perspective of an athlete, George. George was a talented professional football who needed care throughout his life for issues such as substance abuse. Jones (2015, p. 218) considers how George's coaches could have developed a caring approach in their practice and argues, "We want coaches . . . to listen, try to help, look after, look out for and generally act in the best interest of the pupil or athlete."

This is a theme that Knust and Fisher (2015) have developed through their study of exemplary care delivered by 12 female coaches in US collegiate sport. They conclude that these 'exemplary' coaches care by participating in open communication, giving up control to athletes, and modelling care to assistant coaches and athletes. Thus, across these studies and a small number of others not elaborated here (e.g., Fisher, Bejar, Larsen, Fynes, & Gearity, 2017), it appears that coaches in different contexts can and do care through relationships characterised by dialogue, empathy and a concern for another individual.

Noddings' care theory

Consistent with the practice of care through dialogue and a concern for another individual, Noddings' (1984) care ethic has been the dominant theory used by coaching researchers to understand care. For example, all of the earlier studies draw upon Noddings' care ethic, as do other studies of care in coaching (e.g., Gearity, 2012). The roots of Noddings' (1984) care ethic emanates from a feminist perspective on teaching that seeks to put a nurturing, caring relationship at the heart of pedagogical endeavours. This approach is in contrast to what Noddings perceives as depersonalised school systems that have an overemphasis on standardised testing and rigid universal rules at the expense of addressing the holistic needs of learners. Readers may recognise similarities between such school systems and sport programmes that are characterised by competitive outcomes and scientific measurements that dehumanise coach–athlete relationships (Williams & Manley, 2016; Cronin, Whitehead, Webster, & Huntley, 2017). In contrast to such environments, Noddings sees care as an affective and service based ethic that involves teachers acting with and on behalf of the cared for. Indeed, it is this motive to serve the needs of 'the other,' that Noddings argues should underpin all pedagogy. Through this conception of care, Noddings (2014) firmly distinguishes between care as a virtue and care as a relation. For example, care is a virtue for the accountant who is diligently concerned with accuracy and 'carefully' completes a spreadsheet through hard work. On the other hand, Noddings argues that caring for an individual is an affective relation, which requires trust, dialogue and empathy between both individuals. Moreover, Noddings (1984) argues that affective and relational care is underappreciated in pedagogy and wider society.

Noddings' (1984) view of care is heavily influenced by the work of Gilligan (1982). From a feminist perspective, Gilligan argues approaches to relationships, characterised by independence, logical decision making and universally imposed rule-based justice, are generally highly valued in society. Gilligan characterises these relationships as masculine. In contrast, Gilligan asserts that characteristics, which she deems feminine such as nurturing, empathy and maternal servitude, are less valued. To evidence the claim that rule-based relationships are more valued than nurturing care, Gilligan suggests we consider the status and remuneration in wider society that is afforded to professions such as medical doctors, which are associated with scientific approaches. When compared with the financial remuneration afforded to nurses who perform nurturing and empathetic caregiving, we may concede that the rule-based practice is financially more highly rewarded.[1] In another generalised example, we can consider the respect and esteem that wider society affords pre- or primary school teachers[2] who nurture young children. The 'status' afforded to these important carers is often unfavourably contrasted with the university professor who may perform logical scientific research but who may not be involved in affective pastoral care. Undoubtedly, these examples are generalisations, speculations and stereotypes, and, to some extent, Gilligan's arguments do draw too broadly and too simplistically from a wide range of research including Freud and Piaget. Nonetheless, the arguments illustrate Gilligan's gendered assertions that nurturing caring work, which is often performed by women, is at times undervalued and perhaps 'taken for granted.' This might have implications for the gendered world of sport coaching, where female coaches are underrepresented (Norman, 2010).

In response to Gilligan's work, Noddings (1984) sought to re-establish care as a more valued activity. In contrast to Gilligan, however, Noddings (2013) has not advocated a reappraisal of care from a position of gender essentialism wherein women are universally conceived as more or less caring than men. Rather Noddings has declared herself agnostic on this position, arguing that a) appreciating caring relationships as a valuable ethic is justified in its own right, regardless of the gender of the carer and b) that it is through enacting, modelling and developing a caring society that social justice and authentic liberation of marginalised groups will be achieved. To support this conclusion, Noddings positions care as a natural and relational act – e.g., a parent caring for a child. Moreover, she has argued that as children, all individuals are helpless when they enter the world. Thus, Noddings (1984) asserts that it is through interdependent and caring relationships with others (parents, guardians, siblings, teachers) that we ourselves as individuals have flourished. On this basis, Noddings argues that we should all appreciate the care that we have benefited from. This argument leads Noddings to conclude that caring is a relational act, which can positively influence the growth of individuals and the communities they inhabit. In support of this conclusion, and as a result of it, Noddings has produced a substantial body of research work promulgating a care ethic. This work is predominantly, though not exclusively, in areas such as education (Noddings, 2005), on social issues such as homelessness (Noddings, 2002a) and on broader social policy (Noddings, 2002b). In reconceptualising ethics from a caring position and in exploring care across a range of contexts, Noddings has thus established a reputation as a key care theorist. It is therefore, not surprising that when coaching researchers (e.g., Annerstedt & Eva-Carin, 2014; Jones, 2009) have sought to understand care that they have turned to Noddings work and her key concepts.

Noddings' theoretical concepts

Noddings' (1988, p. 219) ethic of care, promulgates a maternal approach which urges those providing care to show devotion through a "total presence to the other" and a desire to serve the "needs, wants and initiations of the second." More succinctly, a carer should "feel with the other and acts in his (sic) behalf" (Noddings, 1988, p. 219). This characterisation of caring illustrates two key concepts that Noddings uses to define care, engrossment and motivational displacement.

Firstly, 'engrossment' is a term used by Noddings (1984) to describe a carer who focuses attention on the 'cared for.' Not surprisingly, given the influence of Gilligan (1982), gendered language is important to Noddings, and she is not entirely satisfied with the term attention as a definition of engrossment. She elaborates that engrossment refers to a specific form of attention that is *repeatedly* focused on the needs of the cared for (Noddings, 2010a). In this way, Noddings suggests caring requires a sustained and committed form of concern and focus. In addition, Noddings (2010b) argues that this concerted attention needs to be receptive and empathetic. This requires carers to engage in authentic listening and observing, where they are open to receiving and understanding the perspective of the cared for. Carers are thus required to recognise the feelings of the other and to do so, as far as possible, without concern for their own agenda. Engrossment therefore requires a form of attention that is committed, empathetic and genuinely open to discovering the experiences, feelings and perspective of the cared for individual.

Secondly, motivational displacement is a concept, which emanates from engrossment. Through engrossment (sustained, empathetic attention), carers will come to know and understand the needs and wants of the cared for. It is also possible, though not inevitable, that carers, will sympathetically experience similar feelings to the cared for. Indeed, these feelings, and/or the empathetic understanding that carers have gained through engrossment, may move carers to put aside their own interests temporarily and act on behalf of the carer. In doing so, the motivation of carers is displaced from serving their own needs to serving the needs of the cared for (Nodding, 2010a). Thus, to care not only requires a sustained form of empathetic attention (engrossment) but also requires a commitment to partition one's own needs and to act in the interests of the cared for (motivational displacement). In addition, care also requires the carer to have the resources and competence (i.e. capacity) to care. Of course, from an ethical perspective, a dilemma may arise where the wants of a cared for individual may alarm, disgust or perhaps simply be too complicated for carers. In such instances, Noddings (2010a) urges us not to harm the cared for, but to listen to their needs (engrossment) and to act in a manner that aims to move the cared for in a different healthier direction (motivational displacement). Thus, even in circumstances, which are complicated, Noddings (2010a) maintains that we care through engrossment and motivational displacement.

Noddings (2007) is also keen to stress that care is a reciprocal relation. By this Noddings argues that a caring relationship requires the 'cared for' to contribute to the relationship and to the carer. At a basic level, this contribution may be as simple as a smile or a thank you. Such actions acknowledge the care offered by a carer and confirm that it has been received by the cared for. Alternatively, the cared for, may act upon or in accordance with advice provided by the carer. In doing so, the cared for illustrates a sense of gratitude and acceptance that may imbue the carer with further motivation. Indeed, without such acceptance, it would be very difficult for carers such as coaches to engage continuously with athletes who do not acknowledge or receive their care. Moreover, by acknowledging care, the cared for (athletes) can provide carers (coaches) with a sense of satisfaction because their care has been deemed relevant and helpful. Thus, although the contribution of the cared for may be less than that provided by carers, for Noddings (2007), care is nonetheless a relationship which both partners contribute to.

Noddings' conception of care as a reciprocal relationship based upon engrossment and motivational displacement has much in common with extant understanding of the coach–athlete relationship. For example, with a humanistic approach in mind, authors, such as Cassidy (2010) and Kidman and Lombardo (2010), have argued that coach–athlete relationships should be empowering of athletes. Other authors have also highlighted how coach–athlete relationships benefit from dialogue, commitment to each other and are dyadic and affective (Jowett, 2007). More recently, athletes and coaches in a community sport setting have highlighted how care through dialogue, empathy and concern can enhance sporting experiences (Cronin, Walsh, Quayle, Whittaker, & Whitehead, 2018). Noddings' relational conception of care and in particular the three concepts of engrossment, motivational displacement and reciprocity thus appear to have much in common and much to add to understanding of the coach–athlete relationships. That said, it is important to note that much sociologically informed research has argued that coach–athlete relationships occur in situated contexts (Jones & Wallace, 2006; Jones, Potrac, Cushion, & Ronglan, 2011; Miller & Cronin, 2013; Cronin & Armour, 2017). From this perspective, it is important to note that although care may occur through interdependent dyadic relationships, these relationships are also situated within dynamic and complex social climates. With this in mind, Newton, Fry and colleagues (2007) have introduced the notion of caring climate as a means of considering how coaches can and should care in sporting environments.

Caring climate: expanding caring concepts to the community

Newton, Fry and colleagues (2007, p. 70) defined the caring climate to be "the extent to which individuals perceive a particular setting to be interpersonally inviting, safe, supportive and able to provide the experience of being valued and respected." These researchers adopted a broad definition of the caring climate to capture both the caring relationship and the concepts of a caring community. The decision to broaden the notion of caring beyond a dyadic relationship was informed by care theory (Noddings, 1992, 2003), the caring school community within the Child Development Project (Battistich, Solomon, Watson, & Schaps, 1997; Battistich, Watson, Solomon, Lewis, & Schaps, 1999) and the Teaching Personal and Social Responsibility (TPSR) model (Hellison, 2011).

While the caring relationship described by Noddings (2003) can be seen as a relationship that occurs between a carer and the cared for, Noddings (1992) does suggest that caring relations can exist within classrooms and among classmates. For example, Noddings (1992) noted that within the classroom, students can be provided opportunities for caring about ideas, caring about others and caring about the environment that extends beyond the caring relation. This has interesting parallels for coaches who may see caring between teammates and within teams and clubs.

Extending caring beyond the interpersonal relationship also underpinned work on caring school communities (Battistich, 2008; Battistich et al., 1997; Battistich et al., 1999). Using other theoretical and conceptual frameworks couched in motivation and social-emotional learning, Battistich and colleagues embarked on the Child Development Project to develop caring school communities. The caring school community was based upon meeting the needs and interests of students through interpersonal relationships – i.e., getting to know each student and adapting instruction to meet their needs. However, a critical component to developing a caring school community was the recognition that fulfilling student needs could not be achieved solely within an individual relationship, but rather that "these needs are given their meaning by, and must be fulfilled in, a group setting" (Battistich et al., 1997, pp. 137–138). Thus, Battistich and colleagues (1997, p. 137) defined these communities:

> as places where members care about and support each other, actively participate in and have influence on the group's activities and decisions, feel a sense of belonging and identification with the group, and have common norms, goals and values.

Through their programme, Battistich and his colleagues sought to create caring school communities by building caring relationships where individuals trusted others, felt safe and respected and demonstrated concern for others. Individuals, and not just teachers, were encouraged to care about one another and be respectful and kind to one another as they live within the school community. Teachers supported these aims by teaching and encouraging students to use social and emotional skills, to help others, to accept help from others and to uphold the norms of the caring community by developing rituals and routines, reinforcing the norms and using caring discipline practices. Finally, teachers modelled positive behaviour, dialogued about caring and other ethical concepts, used collaborative approaches to learning, and encouraged community decision making. This caring community began in the classroom; however, Battistich and colleagues (1997) noted that it extended beyond the teacher and students to include school staff and parents. Therefore, the notion of a caring community entailed both interpersonal dyadic caring relationships as well as supporting and nurturing caring behaviours within a wider community network.

Newton, Fry and colleagues (2007), recognised that the concept of the caring relation or caring school community had parallels with Hellison's (1978, 2011) Teaching and Personal Social Responsibility Model (TPSR). The TPSR model embraces a holistic approach to teaching and coaching, which embodies the caring school community concept. Through his model, Hellison (2011) describes the importance of teaching, discussing, modelling and practicing caring, respectful and cooperative behaviours with programme participants. Further, Hellison espouses a relational focus encouraging teachers and coaches to listen to each person, appreciate them as individuals, recognise their potential and empower them to engage in decision making.

Newton and her colleagues hoped to contribute further to the understanding of caring within physical activity settings. Their research agenda focused on assessing how caring climates could facilitate positive outcomes among young people and exploring how coaches could enact a caring sport community. This endeavour began with intervention work that Doris Watson and Maria Newton were conducting with the National Youth Sport Programme (NYSP). They were implementing TPSR grounded in the caring school community framework.

The caring curriculum included teaching cooperative learning activities and non-traditional sports throughout the camp experience to promote teachable moments and collaboration among campers. The programme also included a leadership training programme designed to promote a caring community. During the training, leaders were encouraged to get to know all children in their group, listen to and respond to their needs and concerns, model respectful and caring behaviour and reinforce caring behaviour that occurred throughout the sport camp (e.g., highlighting a child engaging in caring behaviour at the end of each day of camp). Newton, Watson and colleagues (2007) assessed the effectiveness of this programme in comparison to a traditional NYSP summer sport camp. The youth exposed to the caring NYSP perceived higher levels of caring, reported greater empathetic concern and indicated they would be more likely to participate in the programme the next summer. These conclusions have important implications for coaches in community settings.

This work continued as researchers examined relationships between perceptions of the caring climate and youth development outcomes. From a motivational perspective, a perceived caring climate was positively associated with sport enjoyment, continued participation and sport commitment (Fry & Gano-Overway, 2010; Newton, Fry et al., 2007). With regard to social and emotional outcomes, a perceived caring climate was positively associated with empathy, prosocial behaviours, hope and happiness, and negatively related with antisocial behaviour, sadness and depression (Fry et al., 2012; Gano-Overway et al., 2009).

As research has continued in this area, investigators have examined the caring climate along with the task-involving motivational climate. Reinforcing previous work, a caring climate was positively associated with sport commitment at an individual level among high school athletes (Hall, Newland, Newton, Podlog, & Baucom, 2017). However, research also demonstrates new connections and provides further insight into the climate. For instance, Hogue, Fry, Fry, and Pressman (2013) explored how stress, enjoyment and effort would be impacted when individuals were placed in differing climates (i.e., a caring/task-involving climate and an ego-involving climate) during a 30-minute juggling unit. For the caring component of the intervention, instructors were encouraged to get to know all participants through an opening icebreaker and individual interactions, provide supportive and instructional feedback to individual participants and encourage participants to work together to improve their group juggling time through team challenges and peer coaching. Those exposed to the caring and task-involving climate intervention had lower cortisol levels, higher levels of enjoyment and self-confidence and reported greater effort during the activity, compared to those subjected to an ego-involving climate. Again, these findings have important implications for coaches.

In addition to this quantitative work, qualitative and conceptual work has been conducted to further elucidate aspects of the caring climate in the sport setting. Fry (2010) outlined strategies for creating a welcoming first day to a team, creating opportunities for athletes to get to know and support one another during games and practices and encouraging parents to get to know all players. Claunch and Fry (2016), in collaborating with American Football coaches to build a caring and task-involving climate, described the relational strategies coaches found most useful to their coaching practice. These strategies included getting to know their players and treating them as human beings (rather than just athletes), opening lines of communication and listening to their athletes, understanding their perspective and being respectful. Gano-Overway (2014), building on the concept of *ubuntu*, further encouraged creating a caring community by suggesting coaches develop and reinforce team norms around caring through rituals, routines and shared stories; build harmony and solidarity where players are encouraged to support one another and the team; and empower athletes through consensus building and community decision making. In doing so, this work on coaching climate has illustrated that care can be developed not solely through a Noddings' influenced dyadic relationship, but through a web of caring relationships which contributes to the development of a wider coaching climate. Such climates appear to help athletes flourish, both within and outside of sporting settings.

Limitations of Noddings' care theory

To summarise thus far, it appears that Noddings' work has been a useful aid for coaching researchers aiming to understand care in sporting contexts and aiming to promulgate more caring environments. Notwithstanding this progress, it is important to recognise that care in coaching remains an underdeveloped area. Any theoretical framework used at this early juncture should therefore be subject to critical consideration. To that end, there are several criticisms of Noddings' work that need to be highlighted.

Firstly, although Noddings regularly acknowledges *'caring about'* as an emotional form of concern within her work (e.g., Noddings, 2007), she primarily focuses on advocating a nurturing *'caring for'* approach characterised by engrossment, motivational displacement, and empathy (Noddings, 2013). This predominate focus on a single form of care which is construed as maternal and nurturing perhaps limits appreciation for other forms of care. For example, Knust and Fisher (2015) suggested that in high-performance sport contexts, coaches may care through 'tough love' that may be construed as paternalistic rather than the maternal approach advocated by Noddings. Thus, moving beyond Noddings' focus on caring through nurturing servitude, and with a pluralistic notion of care in mind, Chapter 5 (Terry's story) asks questions about whether coaches can care through logical science based activities.

Secondly, building upon research into caring climate, it is important to recognise that care occurs within a wider social context that is reciprocally shaped by others beyond the carer–cared for dyad (Engster, 2009). This concept is explored in Chapter 4 (Jane's story), which considers how care is conceived and (under)valued in sport contexts. Similarly, on the theme of care as a situated act, Chapter 6 considers how coaches can work with others within sporting environments – e.g., medical professionals to enact care. The chapter also considers if extant coach education empowers and upskills coaches to care for participants or whether other professionals should perform caring in sport.

Finally, Noddings' work has been criticised for not considering the needs of carers themselves (Hoagland, 1990). This is not to say that Noddings does not consider self-care as a concept. Rather it has been argued that she does so only as a means of enabling carers to care for others (Hoagland, 1990). This is a concern, because the concepts of engrossment and motivational displacement can be construed as emotionally laborious and may have ramifications for coaches seeking to care in this manner (Engster, 2009). Accordingly, Chapter 7 (Dave's story) considers care as an emotional labour and how coaches can care for themselves.

To conclude, this chapter has positioned Noddings as the dominant care theorist that has influenced coaching research. The key concepts that underpin Noddings' relational conception of care, such as engrossment, motivational displacement and reciprocity, have been introduced and explained. In addition, work (e.g. Gano-Overway, 2014), which extends Noddings' dyadic notion of care to a more situated climate perspective has also been introduced. Moreover, three key limitations of Noddings' care theory have been outlined with links made to the forthcoming case study chapters that further problematise these limitations. Indeed, in the remainder of this book, the theoretical concepts presented are situated in the contextualised lives of case study coaches with the aim of developing new caring guidelines for coaching researchers, educators and coaches themselves.

Notes

1 This may be a Western European perspective.
2 Akin to kindergarten or elementary school.

Bibliography

Annerstedt, C., & Eva-Carin, L. (2014). Caring as an important foundation in coaching for social sustainability: A case study of a successful Swedish coach in high-performance sport. *Reflective Practice, 15*(1), 27–39. doi:10.1080/14623943.2013.869204

Battistich, V. (2008). Voices: A practitioner's perspective: Character education, prevention, and positive youth development. *Journal of Research in Character Education, 6*(2), 81–90.

Battistich, V., Solomon, D., Watson, M., & Schaps, E. (1997). Caring school communities. *Educational Psychologist, 32*(3), 137–151. doi:10.1207/s15326985ep3203_1

Battistich, V., Watson, M., Solomon, D., Lewis, C., & Schaps, E. (1999). Beyond the three R's: A broader agenda for school reform. *The Elementary School Journal, 99*(1), 415–432. doi:10.1086/461933

Cassidy, T. (2010). Coaching insights: Holism in sports coaching: Beyond humanistic psychology. *International Journal of Sports Science and Coaching, 5*(4), 439–443. doi:10.1260/1747-9541.5.4.439

Claunch, J. L., & Fry, M. D. (2016). Native American football coaches' experience of a motivational climate collaboration with sport psychology researchers. *International Journal of Sports Science & Coaching, 11*(4), 482–495. doi:10.1177/1747954116655047

Cronin, C., & Armour, K. M. (2017). 'Being' in the coaching world: New insights on youth performance coaching from an interpretative phenomenological approach. *Sport, Education and Society, 22*(8), 919–931. doi:10.1080/13573322.2015.1108912

Cronin, C., Walsh, B., Quayle, L., Whittaker, E., & Whitehead, A. (2018). Carefully supporting autonomy: Learning coaching lessons and advancing theory from women's netball in England. *Sports Coaching Review,* 1–23. doi:10.1080/21640629.2018.1429113

Cronin, C., Whitehead, A. E., Webster, S., & Huntley, T. (2017). Transforming, storing and consuming athletic experiences: A coach's narrative of using a video application. *Sport, Education and Society,* 1–13. doi:10.1080/13573322.2017.1355784

Engster, D. (2009). Rethinking care theory: The practice of caring and the obligation to care. *Hypatia, 20*(3), 50–74. doi:10.1111/j.1527-2001.2005.tb00486.x

Fisher, L. A., Bejar, M. P., Larsen, L. K., Fynes, J. M., & Gearity, B. T. (2017). Caring in U.S. National Collegiate Athletic Association division 1 sport: The perspectives of 18 female and male head coaches. *International Journal of Sports Science and Coaching, 12*(1), 75–91. doi:10.1177/1747954116684388

Fry, M. D. (2010). Creating a positive climate for young athletes from day 1. *Journal of Sport Psychology in Action, 1*(1), 33–41. doi:10.1080/21520704.2010.518224

Fry, M. D., & Gano-Overway, L. (2010). Exploring the contribution of the caring climate to the youth sport experience. *Journal of Applied Sport Psychology, 22*(3), 294–304. doi:10.1080/10413201003776352

Fry, M. D., Guivernau, M., Kim, M. S., Newton, M., Gano-Overway, L. A., & Magyar, T. M. (2012). Youth perceptions of a caring climate, emotional regulation, and psychological well-being. *Sport, Exercise, and Performance Psychology, 1*(1), 44–57. doi:10.1037/a0025454

Gano-Overway, L. A. (2014). The caring climate: How sport environments can develop empathy in young people. In K. Pavlovich, & K. Krahnke (Eds.), *Organising through empathy* (pp. 166–183). New York, NY: Routledge.

Gano-Overway, L. A., Newton, M., Magyar, T. M., Fry, M. D., Kim, M. S., & Guivernau, M. R. (2009). Influence of caring youth sport contexts on efficacy-related beliefs and social behaviors. *Developmental Psychology, 45*(2), 329–340. doi:10.1037/a0014067

Gearity, B. (2012). Coach as unfair and uncaring. *Journal for the Study of Sports and Athletes in Education, 6*(2), 173–200. doi:10.1179/ssa.2012.6.2.173

Gilligan, C. (1982). *In a different voice.* Boston, MA: Harvard.

Hall, M. S., Newland, A., Newton, M., Podlog, L., & Baucom, B. R. (2017). Perceptions of the social psychological climate and sport commitment in adolescent athletes: A multilevel analysis. *Journal of Applied Sport Psychology, 29*(1), 75–87. doi:10.1080/10413200.2016.1174906

Hellison, D. R. (1978). *Beyond balls and bats: Alienated (and other) youth in the gym.* Washington, DC: AAHPER Publications Sales.

Hellison, D. R. (2011). *Teaching personal and social responsibility through physical activity.* Champaign, IL: Human Kinetics.

Hoagland, S. L. (1990). Some concerns about Nel Noddings' 'caring'. *Hypatia, 5*(1), 109–114. doi:10.1111/j.1527-2001.1990.tb00394.x

Hogue, C. M., Fry, M. D., Fry, A. C., & Pressman, S. D. (2013). The influence of a motivational climate intervention on participants' salivary cortisol and psychological responses. *Journal of Sport and Exercise Psychology, 35*(1), 85–97. doi:10.1123/jsep.35.1.85

Jones, C. (2015). Care and phronesis in teaching and coaching: Dealing with personality. *Sport, Education and Society.* doi:10.1080/13573322.2015.1015976

Jones, R. L. (2009). Coaching as caring (the smiling gallery): Accessing hidden knowledge. *Physical Education and Sport Pedagogy, 14*(4), 377–390. doi:10.1080/17408980801976551

Jones, R. L., Potrac, P., Cushion, C., & Ronglan, L. (2011). *The sociology of sports coaching.* London: Routledge.

Jones, R. L., & Wallace, M. (2006). The coach as 'orchestrator': More realistically managing the complex coaching context. In R. L. Jones (Ed.), *The sports coach as educator: Re-conceptualising sports coaching* (pp. 51–64). London: Routledge.

Jowett, S. (2007). Interdependence analysis and the 3 + 1 Cs in the coach-athlete relationship. In S. Jowett, D. Lavallee, S. Jowett, & D. Lavallee (Eds.), *Social psychology in sport* (pp. 15–27). Champaign, IL: Human Kinetics.

Kidman, L., & Lombardo, B. (2010). *Athlete-centred coaching: Developing decision makers* (2nd ed.). Worcester, MA: IPC Print Resources.

Knust, S. K., & Fisher, L. A. (2015). NCAA division I female head coaches' experiences of exemplary care within coaching. *International Sport Coaching Journal, 2*(2), 94–107. doi:10.1123/iscj.2013-0045

Miller, P. K., & Cronin, C. (2013). Rethinking the factuality of 'contextual' factors in an ethnomethodological mode: Towards a reflexive understanding of action-context dynamism in the theorization of coaching. *Sports Coaching Review, 1*(2), 106–123. doi:10.1080/21640629.2013.790166

Newton, M., Fry, M., Watson, D., Gano-Overway, L., Kim, M. S., Magyar, M., & Guivernau, M. (2007). Psychometric properties of the caring climate scale in a physical activity setting. *Revista de Psicología del Deporte, 16*(1), 67–84.

Noddings, N. (1984). *Caring: A feminine approach to ethics and moral education*. Berkeley, CA: University of California Press.

Noddings, N. (1988). An ethic of caring and its implications for instructional arrangements. *American Journal of Education, 96*(2), 215–230. doi:10.1086/443894

Noddings, N. (1992). *The challenge to care in schools: An alternative approach to education*. New York, NY: Teachers College Press.

Noddings, N. (2002a). Caring, social policy and homelessness. *Theoretical Medicine and Bioethics, 23*(6), 441–454.

Noddings, N. (2002b). *Starting at home: Caring and social policy*. London: University of California Press.

Noddings, N. (2003). *Caring: A feminine approach to ethics and moral education*. Berkeley, CA: University of California Press.

Noddings, N. (2005). *The challenge to care in schools: An alternative approach to education* (2nd ed.). New York, NY: Teachers College Press.

Noddings, N. (2007). Caring as relation and virtue in teaching. In R. L. Walker, & P. J. Ivanhoe (Eds.), *Working virtue: Virtue ethics and contemporary moral problems* (pp. 41–60). Oxford: Oxford University Press.

Noddings, N. (2010a). Complexity in caring and empathy. *Abstracta, 6*(2), 6–12.

Noddings, N. (2010b). *The maternal factor: Two paths to morality*. Berkeley, CA: University of California Press.

Noddings, N. (2013). *Caring; A relational approach to ethics and moral education* (2nd ed.). London: University of California Press.

Noddings, N. (2014). *Caring in education*. Retrieved from http://infed.org/mobi/caring-in-education/

Norman, L. (2010). Feeling second best: Elite women coaches' experiences. *Sociology of Sport Journal, 27*(1), 89–104.

Williams, S., & Manley, A. (2016). Elite coaching and the technocratic engineer: Thanking the boys at Microsoft! *Sport, Education and Society, 21*(6), 828–850. doi:10.1080/13573322.2014.958816

3 Why pedagogical case studies?

Kathleen Armour and Colum Cronin

What is a pedagogical case?

'Caring' is an inherently holistic pedagogical and personal activity. As such, caring in coaching is an ideal topic around which to develop 'pedagogical cases.' The concept of a pedagogical case originates with Armour's (2014) work in PE and youth sport. In its first iteration, a pedagogical case was defined as both a translational research mechanism and a professional learning tool. The ambition was to develop a new mechanism that would help to bridge persisting research/theory/practice gaps by offering a different way in which teaching/coaching practitioners and researchers could engage and learn collaboratively. The overarching aim was to provide rich information that could enable practitioners and researchers to better understand and meet the needs of individual young learners.

In that first iteration, 20 pedagogical cases were constructed by multidisciplinary teams of authors working together to analyse the learning needs of a single young person in a PE or sport setting. The framework for each pedagogical case was as follows:

1 Case narrative about a learner (a child or young person) written by the case team drawing on their collective experience
2 Multidisciplinary perspectives (usually three) on the case narrative
3 Pedagogical perspective that attempted to draw the strands together to generate new, interdisciplinary knowledge

The pedagogical cases model has since been adapted to focus on PE teachers and the ways in which they use digital technologies in their teaching (Casey, Goodyear, & Armour, 2016) and young people engaging with social media to find health-related information (Goodyear & Armour, in press). In each of these later versions, the original pedagogical cases model has been enhanced. For example, in Casey et al. (2016), the teachers wrote the narratives at the heart of the cases and then also wrote a reflection on the whole pedagogical case once it was completed. In Goodyear and Armour (in press), the cases were structured around composite narratives constructed from a large data set generated from a research project investigating young people, social media and health. The important point to make, therefore, is that the pedagogical cases framework was always designed to be used as a guide rather than a rigid blueprint.

In this book, the pedagogical cases are described as 'caring cases.' Similar to Casey et al. (2016), the case studies focus on pedagogical practice from the perspective of practitioners. The coaches themselves and the contexts in which they practice are described at the beginning of each case study chapter. Following these descriptions, incidents of coaching practice are narrated. The narrations utilise the voices of coaches (indented) to situate incidents in the everyday experiences of coaches. Each narrative is accompanied by analyses from distinct disciplinary perspectives (e.g. sociology, pedagogy, psychology, physiology). These multidisciplinary analyses are in keeping with the approach taken in Casey et al. (2016) and indeed, the original pedagogical cases concept (Armour, 2014). The pedagogical cases model has, however, also been adapted here. Specifically, both the incidents described by the coaches and the accompanying analyses are focused on care and caring practices. Thus, caring practice serves as an original framework for the narratives and analysis. As a result of this framework, each chapter provides situated accounts of practice and multidisciplinary analyses, which illuminate our understanding of care. The cases therefore offer a useful pedagogical tool, which can help readers to connect coaching practice with care theory and vice versa.

The original inspiration for the pedagogical cases model came from the realisation that in PE and youth sport – as in education more broadly – there are limiting and enduring gaps between theory and practice, researchers and practitioners, and between sub-disciplines of our core underpinning academic fields. It is difficult to explain fully or justify these gaps given that researchers claim to be conducting research to inform better practice, and sub/disciplinary researchers claim to have unique insights from their own disciplinary lenses into understanding practice. Yet the practitioners – teachers and coaches – are rarely engaged in selecting topics for research or designing and conducting that research. Moreover, the outputs of much research in the highly relevant fields of education/pedagogy and sport sciences/kinesiology are often inaccessible to practitioners as a result of the style of the reporting or the medium in which it is published. Hence, pedagogical cases are an attempt to develop a new mechanism to bridge these persistent gaps.

In the first pedagogical cases book, a call to action in the broad field of education was presented as a major justification for attempting to develop a new translational research mechanism:

> In her Presidential Address to the 2012 American Educational Research Association (AERA), Arnetha Ball challenged researchers to "move away from research designed as mere 'demonstrations of knowledge' towards research that has the power to close the knowing-doing gap in education" (Ball, 2012, p. 283). Ball argued passionately that although it is important for researchers in education to conduct research that can create new knowledge, "to know is not enough" because knowing "is not sufficient to address social problems, mitigate inequalities, or advance innovative methods of instruction" (p. 284). Noting also that "there is a gap between what we know and what is widely done in the educational arena" (p. 285) Ball made a case for more translational research to close persisting knowledge-practice or research-practice gaps. She argued that what is required is "persistent, collaborative and generative work" (p. 285) and "resources and mechanisms to promote the use of research to improve education" (p. 292).
>
> (Armour, 2014, p. 7)

Of course, this is not a simple task. The concept of 'translation' is contested, suggesting, as it does, that research should be translated into practice rather than co-constructed with practitioners. The idea that researchers can conduct their research on 'subjects' and then simply deliver the research findings to relevant stakeholders who will act on the results has long been discredited (Oakes, 2017). In this book, therefore, coaches were front and centre in the research process, and their narratives have driven the focus on caring in sport coaching. It has also been widely reported that traditional forms of professional development for coaches often fail to meet their needs (Armour, Quennerstedt, Chambers, & Makopoulou, 2017; Griffiths, Armour, & Cushion, 2017). This leaves practitioners to draw heavily on their personal experiences rather than the wider perspectives they might need to make sense of the many different learners in front of them. In the context of any educational activity, Akkerman and Van Eijck (2013, p. 60) argued, "The learner should be approached . . . as a whole person who participates in school as well as in many other practices." A pedagogical cases approach is an attempt, therefore, to position the central figure in the case (the coach) holistically in order to better learn with and from their experiences.

It is worth breaking down the term 'pedagogical cases' into its two constituent parts. *Pedagogy* is a contested term and is certainly so in the field of sport pedagogy (Tinning, 2008; Kirk & Stolz, 2015). In an earlier book (Armour, 2011), sport pedagogy was defined as a three dimensional concept whose dimensions were made even more complex in their interaction in each pedagogical encounter. The three dimensions were knowledge in context, learners and learning and teachers/ teaching and coaches coaching (p. 3). The cases within this book, incorporate all three elements. *Case study* is a widely used research method, but it is also widely challenged. Stenhouse (1979, p. 4) argued strongly for the value of case studies to support practitioner learning, and Stake (2000) has provided extensive literature on the many dimensions of case study research. The critiques of case study as method focus on the tendency for descriptive narratives, small sample sizes and the impossibility of generalisability in the traditional research sense. Yet, as Thomas (2011, preface) pointed out, "at its best, case study provides the most vivid, the most inspirational analysis that inquiry can offer."

While not claiming that the pedagogical cases presented in this book are the 'the most' inspirational, we would claim that they offer unique insights into the everyday complex human activity that is pedagogy in a coaching context. In that sense, they are perhaps more relevant to the commonplace experiences of practitioners. In Shulman's (1987) classic classification of the seven forms of knowledge required for teaching, he identified two elements that are particularly pertinent to this book: knowledge of learners and their characteristics and knowledge of educational contexts and of educational ends, purposes and values. These two elements alone – even without the other five – are challenging, suggesting, as they do, a broad and holistic understanding of learners, learning and wider context. Thus, it is, that the sheer complexity of each pedagogical encounter is signalled. As Armour (2014) argued:

> This point is one of the cornerstones of the concept of pedagogical cases. Academics and researchers can choose – indeed, are often encouraged – to focus on specialised fields of study and specific disciplines or sub-disciplines. Yet, for practitioners in physical education and youth sport, this high degree of specialisation is simply not feasible. If practice is to be informed and effective (i.e. 'professional') then teaching or coaching a group of children will require knowledge of a range of human movement sciences, social sciences including education, aspects of the humanities and technical knowledge. Added to this is a need to understand how all of this knowledge applies to a specific group of young learners and the different individuals within that group. In other words, the cognitive challenge *alone* for the professional practitioner is daunting.

This rationale explains the attempt made in this book to focus on understanding and illustrating caring as a core coaching activity, while analysing it further from a range of disciplinary perspectives. Essentially, if we as academics from our positions of expertise are unable to offer each other and accept new insights that can inform our preferred theories, methods and research practices, we will have little to offer practitioners for whom daily practice is extraordinarily complex. On this note, it is worth remembering that practice is *always* not only multidisciplinary but also interdisciplinary (for further discussion see Armour, 2014).

How were the cases developed?

In order to prioritise the voices of coaches, and to situate the narratives in contextualised environments, the case studies were constructed using phenomenology. Phenomenological research is based upon a rich history of philosophy that includes, but is not limited to, work by Husserl (1913/1982); Heidegger (1927/2005); Sartre (1943/1984);

and Merleau-Ponty (1962).[1] The roots of this philosophy lie in Husserl's (1900/1973) rejection of positivist psychology, which he felt removed individual lived experience from research, and therefore resulted in dehumanised understandings of phenomenon. In contrast, it was argued that those best placed to understand a phenomenon are those who experience the phenomenon (Husserl, 1913/1982). Thus, Husserl's phenomenology valued subjective experience as a means of explaining the world around us in a more humane, relevant and insightful manner. Since then, researchers inspired by phenomenological philosophy have studied phenomena through the subjective view of individuals (Gray, 2009). This emphasis on subjective interpretation is in stark contrast to traditional (dualistic and positivist) approaches, which at times have sought knowledge, in spite of, rather than through, the subjective interpretations of participants.

The phenomenological tenet that subjective experience is the route to understanding has underpinned studies in a wide range of areas with many in the broad field of health research (Brocki & Wearden, 2006). Typically, these studies involve a) small idiographic sample sizes, b) interviews that invite participants to share their experiences and c) results that include both rich description and insightful analysis of individual experience (Finlay, 2009). In health care, these features have provided understandings of first person experiences such as bereavement, self-injury, dementia and addiction (Brocki & Wearden, 2006).

Sport provides a rich array of subjective experiences, which makes it a productive field for phenomenological research – e.g., participating, coaching, refereeing and spectating (Kerry & Armour, 2000). For example, researchers have used phenomenological approaches to examine athletes' experiences of movement (Brown & Payne, 2009) and physical contact in basketball (Rail, 1990). More recently phenomenological studies have explored participation in golf (Ravn & Christensen, 2014), running and scuba diving (Allen-Collinson & Hockey, 2011) and PE (Standal, 2015; Thorburn & Stolz, 2015; Thorburn, 2008). These phenomenology informed studies have provided insightful, evocative and vivid descriptions of diverse sport experiences. Such accounts are valuable because much coach education research has indicated that coaches can learn from examining their own experiences and the experiences of others (Gilbert & Trudel, 2002; Rynne, Mallet, & Tinning, 2006; Werthner & Trudel, 2009).

In coaching, a small number of studies have also used phenomenological methods. Lundkvist, Gustafsson, Hjälm, and Hassmén (2012) account of burnout in elite coaches, Gearity and Murray's (2011) examination of 'bad coaching' and Becker's (2009) study of athletes' experiences of 'great coaching,' all use phenomenology to explore the subjective experiences of coaches. In keeping with phenomenology, these studies use small sample sizes and gather rich descriptions of coaching experiences. Through analysing the coaches' experiences, the authors have also added new insights into everyday experiences. Most relevant to this book, Cronin and Armour (2017) used phenomenological case studies to identify that care is an essential aspect of coaching practice. Thus, these studies have demonstrated the potential of phenomenology to provide perceptive analyses of sport coaches' everyday practices and care in particular.

Christensen (2009) and Miller, Cronin and Baker (2015) also undertook phenomenological studies that explore the experience of coaches. These studies focus on understanding the essential characteristics of identifying talent, but the studies also recognise that talent identification practices occur within a broader 'lifeworld.' For example, coaches in smaller sports clubs have fewer financial resources, and this influences their ability to provide opportunities for all the athletes that they deem talented. Similarly, in a study of community based sport coaching, Cronin and Armour (2013) used phenomenology to describe the essential characteristics of community sport coaching. This study described the lifeworld of the community coach, which is both hidden (offices and meeting rooms) and public facing (sport centres, schools). In doing so, these studies built upon another phenomenological tenet from Heidegger (1927/2005) who argued that our experiences always occur within, and are reflexively shaped by, an interpersonal and social lifeworld. This is important because as illustrated in Chapter 1, coaching is increasingly recognised as an interpersonal, dynamic and socially situated concept (Bowes & Jones, 2006; Evans, 2017; Barnson, 2014). Once again, this illustrates the promise of phenomenology for sport coaching research (Kerry & Armour, 2000). To build on this promise, phenomenology was used as part of a larger study (Cronin & Armour, 2017), and as a framework for the case studies in Chapters 4–7, because it a) prioritises the experiences of participants as a route to understanding and b) describes how experiences are reflexively influenced by a social context.

How were the coaches' stories collected?

Phenomenological studies typically involve the recruitment of a small sample of participants and this facilitates the collection of in-depth accounts of experience (Finlay, 2009). Consistent with this convention and following institutional ethical approval, purposeful sampling (Patton, 1990) was used to identify four case study coaches.

(Cronin & Armour, 2017, p. 922)

Three criteria were employed as a means of ensuring that the sample reflected the phenomenological nature of the study (Sparkes & Smith, 2009). The first criterion required participants to have in-depth and recent experiences of the 'phenomenon' – i.e., coaching (Becker, 2009). This criterion is consistent with the phenomenological tenet that the people best placed to elucidate a phenomenon are those that experience it. Secondly, Moustakas (1994) argues that not only must the sample have experience of the phenomenon under investigation but also they must have an interest in exploring the phenomenon alongside the researcher, acting as such, as a variant of co-researcher. Thirdly, the coaches also practiced in a range of contexts including individual and team sports, and with adult and youth athletes.

Given the variety of contexts in which the coaches practice, the sample are well placed to describe care in coaching. It is important to note, however, that although the sample included varied characteristics it is not claimed that the sample is representative of a population. For instance, two of the coaches in the case studies are female, but we do not suggest that they represent *all* female coaches. Neither is it claimed that these are examples of good or bad practice. Rather, these coaches' experiences are interesting in their own right. Indeed, the unique characteristics ensured that each coach was diverse enough to be characterised as a distinct case while also reflecting experiences and viewed that will resonate with a range of readers (Stake, 1995).

Following informed consent, each case study coach provided rich descriptions of incidental accounts of care in coaching during three semi-structured interviews that were conducted as part of a larger study (Cronin & Armour, 2017). Congruent with phenomenology's emphasis on the subjective experience of participants, the interview schedule was composed of open-ended questions that invited participants to tell their stories such as, "'What is a typical coaching experience?' and 'What is it like to walk in your shoes?'" (Cronin & Armour, 2017, p. 923). These questions provided opportunities for participants to focus on their coaching, describe their experiences, and direct the interviews. Following these early questions, each participant was invited to describe their coaching context (lifeworld). During this phase of the interview, the researcher adopted the role of the 'fool' and asked questions to gather rich description (Muller, 2011). Examples of lifeworld questions included the following: "'Who is there when you are coaching?'; 'What are their roles?'; 'What do they do?'" (Cronin & Armour, 2017, p. 923) As interviews progressed, questions reflected hermeneutical (Heidegger, 1927/2005) and existential phenomenological (Sartre, 1943/1984) approaches such as "How do you see yourself as a coach" and "Who and what depends on you?"

How are the cases presented?

Interview data were analysed using phenomenological procedures recommended by Van Manen (1990) and detailed in Cronin and Armour (2017). These procedures involved selecting unique statements in the participants' descriptions that were "particularly revealing about the phenomenon" – i.e., care (Van Manen, 1990, p. 93). The authors then examined meaningful segments. The authors considered whether the segments provided rich incidental accounts of care, and were relevant to the world of the case study coach. If so, meaningful segments were utilised to form the narrative cases studies that follow in Chapters 4–7. Specifically, the meaningful segments were used verbatim to construct a case study.[2] In addition, the authors added narrated content around these segments in order to guide readers through the coaches' own stories.

Narrated stories are an appropriate format to discuss care as Holley and Colyar (2009, p. 200) state, "People can 'apprehend' the world narratively, and people can 'tell' about the world narratively." Similarly, Smith and Sparkes (2008, p. 280) emphasise the value of narratives as:

> opportunities and spaces for people to often tell long, in-depth, rich and contradictory stories about their thoughts, emotions and lives in ways they may not have done previously, and in a manner that quicker and cleaner methods can suppress.

Thus, as readers approach the narrative case studies in Chapters 4–7, we invite them to act as connoisseurs (Sparkes & Smith, 2009) and evaluate whether the case studies provide:

1 First-person accounts of coaching experience;
2 Rich descriptions of the lifeworld in which coaches care; or
3 Insightful analyses that shed light on the phenomenon in question – care.

As pedagogical cases, the aim of the chapters is not merely to present contextualised accounts of coaching practice. Rather, the cases aspire to stimulate theoretical debate and help readers to connect care theory with their own pedagogical practice (Armour, 2014). To that end, the editors then invited co-authors to read and comment on the case from their own disciplinary perspective – i.e., pedagogy, sociology, physiology, psychology and medicine. This is consistent with the pedagogical cases concept that recognises that all physical activity is interdisciplinary (Armour, 2014). Each narrative is therefore, accompanied by two disciplinary analyses that provide theoretical explanation and insight relevant to care. Accordingly, each of the case study chapters includes the following:

1 An introduction to a coach and their coaching context;
2 A narrated description of coaching incidents related to care;
3 An initial analysis of the coaching practice from a caring perspective;
4 Two different disciplinary analyses that consider care within the case; and
5 A concluding section, which considers implications and questions raised from the case.

By taking this approach, we hope that students, coaches, coach educators, coaching researchers and employers can learn more about care; reflect on care in their own practice settings; and find new ways to effect change in their own coaching worlds.

Notes

1 These philosophies are more complex and at times more contradictory than presented here. In the interests of relevance and brevity, the philosophies

are not explored further in this text. Readers interested in the range of phenomenological philosophy should consider exploring Spiegelberg (1994) or Moran (2000).

2 Minor amendments were made to ensure clarity.

Bibliography

Akkerman, S. F., & van Eijck, M. (2013). Re-theorising the student dialogically across and between boundaries of multiple communities. *British Educational Research Journal*, *39*(1), 60–72. Doi:10.1080/01411926.2 011.613454

Allen-Collinson, J., & Hockey, J. (2011). Feeling the way: Notes toward a haptic phenomenology of distance running and scuba diving. *International Review for the Sociology of Sport*, *46*(3), 1–16. Doi:10.1177/ 1012690210380577

Armour, K. M. (2011). *Sport pedagogy: An introduction for teaching and coaching* (1st ed.). London: Routledge.

Armour, K. M. (2014). *Pedagogical cases in physical education and youth sport* (1st ed.). Oxon: Routledge.

Armour, K. M., Quennerstedt, M., Chambers, F. C., & Makopoulou, K. (2017). What is effective CPD for contemporary physical educatio teachers: A deweyan framework. *Sport, Education and Society*, *22*(7), 799–811. Doi:10.1080/13573322.2015.1083000

Barnson, S. C. (2014). Toward a theory of coaching paradox. *Quest*, *66*(4), 371–384. Doi:10.1080/00336297.2014.918891

Becker, A. J. (2009). It's not what they do, it's how they do it: Athlete experiences of great coaching. *International Journal of Sports Science & Coaching*, *4*(1), 93–119. Doi:10.1260/1747-9541.4.1.93

Bowes, I., & Jones, R. L. (2006). Working at the edge of chaos: Understanding coaching as a complex, interpersonal system. *The Sport Psychologist*, *20*(2), 235–245. Doi:10.1123/tsp.20.2.235

Brocki, J. M., & Wearden, A. J. (2006). A critical evaluation of the use of interpretative phenomenological analysis (IPA) in health psychology. *Psychology and Health*, *21*(1), 87–108. Doi:10.1080/14768320500230185

Brown, T. D., & Payne, P. G. (2009). Conceptualizing the phenomenology of movement in physical education: Implications for pedagogical inquiry and development. *Quest*, *61*, 418–441. Doi:10.1080/00336297.2009.10483624

Casey, A., Goodyear, V., & Armour, K. (2016). *Digital technologies and learning in physical education: Pedagogical cases*. London: Routledge.

Christensen, M. K. (2009). "An Eye for Talent": Talent Identification and the "Practical Sense" of Top-Level Soccer Coaches. *Sociology of Sport Journal*, *26*(3), 365–382. doi:10.1123/ssj.26.3.365

Cronin, C., & Armour, K. M. (2013). Lived experience and community sport coaching: A phenomenological investigation. *Sport, Education and Society*. Doi:10.1080/13573322.2013.858625

Cronin, C., & Armour, K. M. (2017). 'Being' in the coaching world: New insights on youth performance coaching from an interpretative phenomenological approach. *Sport, Education and Society*, *22*(8), 919–931. Doi:10.108 0/13573322.2015.1108912

Evans, B. (2017). Sports coaching as action-in-context: Using ethnomethodological conversation analysis to understand the coaching process. *Qualitative Research in Sport, Exercise and Health*, *9*(1), 111–132. Doi: 10.1080/2159676X.2016.1246473

Finlay, L. (2009). Debating phenomenological research methods. *Phenomenology & Practice*, *3*(1), 6–25. Doi:10.1007/978-94-6091-834-6_2

Gearity, B. T., & Murray, M. (2011). Athletes' experiences of the psychological effects of poor coaching. *Psychology of Sport and Exercise*, *12*(3), 213–221. Doi:10.1016/j.psychsport.2010.11.004

Gilbert, W. D., & Trudel, P. (2002). Learning to coach through experience: Reflection in model youth sport coaches. *Journal of Teaching in Physical Education*, *21*(1), 16–34. Doi:10.1123/jtpe.21.1.16

Goodyear, V., & Armour, K. M. (in press). *Young people, social media and health*. London: Routledge.

Gray, D. E. (2009). *Doing research in the real world* (2nd ed.). London: Sage Publication.

Griffiths, M., Armour, K. M., & Cushion, C. (2017). 'Trying to get our message across': Successes and challenges in an evidence-based professional development programme for sport coaches. *Sport, Education and Society*, *23*(3), 283–295. Doi:10.1080/13573322.2016.1182014

Heidegger, M. (1927/2005). *Being and time* (J. Macquarrie, & E. Robinson, Trans.). Oxford: Blackwell.

Holley, K. A., & Colyar, J. (2009). Rethinking texts narrative and the construction of qualitative research. *Educational Researcher*, *38*(9), 680–686. Doi:10.3102/0013189X09351979

Husserl, E. (1900/1973). *Logical investigations* (J. N. Findlay, Trans.). London: Routledge.

Husserl, E. (1913/1982). *Ideas pertaining to a pure phenomenology and to a phenomenological philosophy: First book: General introduction to a pure phenomenology* (F. Kersten, Trans.). The Hague: Nijhoff.

Kerry, D. S., & Armour, K. M. (2000). Sport sciences and the promise of phenomenology: Philosophy, method and insight. *Quest*, *52*(1), 1–17. Doi:10.1080/00336297.2000.10491697

Kirk, D., & Stolz, S. A. (2015). David Kirk on physical education and sport pedagogy: In dialogue with Steven Stolz. *Asia-Pacific Journal of Health,*

Sport and Physical Education, 6(2), 127–142. Doi:10.1080/18377122.2 015.1051265

Lundkvist, E., Gustafsson, H., Hjälm, S., & Hassmén, P. (2012). An interpretative phenomenological analysis of burnout and recovery in elite soccer coaches. *Qualitative Research in Sport, Exercise and Health, 4*, 400–419. Doi:10.1080/2159676X.2012.693526

Merleau-Ponty, M. (1962). *Phenomenology of perception.* London: Routledge.

Miller, P. K., Cronin, C., & Baker, G. (2015). Nurture, nature and some very dubious social skills: An interpretative phenomenological analysis of talent identification practices in elite English youth soccer. *Qualitative Research in Sport, Exercise and Health.* Doi:10.1080/2159676X. 2015.1012544

Moran, D. (2000). *Introduction to phenomenology.* London: Routledge.

Moustakas, C. (1994). *Phenomenological research methods.* London: Sage Publication.

Muller, A. (2011). From phenomenology to existentialism: Philosophical approaches towards sport. *Sport, Ethics and Philosophy, 5*(3), 202–216. Doi:10.1080/17511321.2011.602572

Oakes, J. (2017). 2016 AERA Presidential address public scholarship: Education research for a diverse democracy. *Educational Researcher, 47*(2), 91–104. Doi:0013189X17746402

Patton, M. (1990). *Qualitative evaluation and research methods.* Los Angeles: Sage Publication.

Rail, G. (1990). Physical contact in women's basketball: A first interpretation. *International Review for the Sociology of Sport, 25*(4), 269–285. Doi:10.1177/101269029202700101

Ravn, S., & Christensen, M. (2014). Listening to the body? How phenomenological insights can be used to explore a golfer's experience of the physicality of her body. *Qualitative Research in Sport, Exercise and Health, 6*(4), 462–477. Doi:10.1080/2159676X.2013.809378

Rynne, S., Mallet, C., & Tinning, R. (2006). High performance sport coaching: Institutes of sport as sites for learning. *International Journal of Sports Science and Coaching, 1*(3), 223–234. Doi:10.1260/174795406778604582

Sartre, J.-P. (1943/1984). *Being and nothingness* (H. E. Barnes, Trans.). New York, NY: Washington Square Press.

Shulman, L. (1987). Knowledge and teaching: Foundation of a new reform. *Harvard Review, 57*(1), 1–22. Doi:10.17763/haer.57.1.j463w79r56455411

Smith, B., & Sparkes, A. (2008). Contrasting perspectives on narrating selves and identities: An invitation to dialogue. *Qualitative Research, 8*(1), 5–35. Doi:10.1177/1468794107085221

Sparkes, A. C., & Smith, B. (2009). Judging the quality of qualitative inquiry: Criteriology and relativism in action. *Psychology of Sport and Exercise, 10*(5), 491–497. Doi:10.1016/j.psychsport.2009.02.006

Spiegelberg, H. (1994). *The phenomenological movement*. London: Kluwer Academic Publishers.

Stake, R. E. (1995). *The art of case study research*. London: Sage Publication.

Stake, R. E. (2000). Case studies. In N. K. Denzin, & Y. S. Lincoln (Eds.), *Handbook of qualitative research* (pp. 435–455). London: Sage Publication.

Standal, O. F. (2015). *Phenomenology and pedagogy in physical education* (1st ed.). Oxon: Routledge.

Stenhouse, L. (1979). Case study in comparative education: Particularity and generalisation. *Comparative Education, 15*(1), 5–10. Doi:10.1080/0305006790150102

Thomas, G. (2011). A typology for the case study in social science following a review of definition, discourse, and structure. *Qualitative Inquiry, 17*(6), 511–521. Doi:10.1177/1077800411409884

Thorburn, M. (2008). Articulating a Merleau-Pontian phenomenology of physical education: The quest for active student engagement and authentic assessment in high-stakes examination awards. *European Physical Education Review, 14*(2), 263–280. Doi:10.1177/1356336X08090709

Thorburn, M., & Stolz, S. (2015). Embodied learning and school-based physical culture: Implications for professionalism and practice in physical education. *Sport, Education and Society*. http://dx.doi.org/10.1080/13573322.2015.1063993

Tinning, R. (2008). Pedagogy, sport pedagogy, and the field of kinesiology. *Quest, 60*(3), 405–424. Doi:10.1080/00336297.2008.10483589

Van Manen, M. (1990). *Researching lived experience*. London: University of Western Ontario.

Werthner, P., & Trudel, P. (2009). Investigating the idiosyncratic learning paths of elite canadian coaches. *International Journal of Sports Science & Coaching, 4*(3), 433–449. Doi:10.1260/174795409789623946

4 Nurturing care in sport coaching

Jane's story

Colum Cronin and Kathleen Armour

In my (Colum) coaching role, the time I spend on the training pitch, gym or court can sometimes feel like the easiest part of my day. In contrast, the time I spend 'off the field' on buses, at meetings and in hotels with staff, athletes and parents can be physically, intellectually and emotionally draining. I do not enjoy this 'off the field' work, even though I recognise it is an essential part of my coaching role. Interestingly, most coaching manuals and – to a large extent – coaching research fails to account for the work coaches do away from the field of play, so I and other coaches have little support available to help me to develop this part of my role.

Jane's story is different. It fills a gap in our knowledge about coaching by illustrating that coaching practice does not finish with the final whistle; instead it is an ongoing process that continues into conversations with numerous others such as parents, fellow staff and athletes. More specifically, Jane's story demonstrates how coaches can use off the field time to care for athletes in a dialogical and maternal manner. This is aligned to Noddings' (2005) two key concepts (discussed in Chapter 2):

1   Engrossment – where coaches seek to understand fully the needs of the athlete; and
2   Motivational displacement – where coaches' actions are in response to the athletes' rather than the coaches' needs.

Jane's story also illustrates that she lives a busy coaching life. This means she has to consider how best to spend her time and energy: should she use her time to care for athletes, her sport or her career, and how does care for her own family fit in? To illustrate these questions, Jane's story is organised into four sections, the first three of which draw extensively on data from a series of interviews with Jane (discussed previously in Chapter 3). The first section introduces Jane as a person including a short biography and an overview of some key contextual issues that were discussed in our interviews. The next two sections consist of theoretically informed perspectives on Jane's narrative. The first perspective draws on pedagogical literature to consider how Jane cares in ways, which are consistent with Noddings' (2005) ethical notion of care. The second perspective introduces the sociologically informed concepts of 'care full lives,' and 'care ceiling' (Grummell, Devine, & Lynch, 2009). Taken as a whole, it is apparent that Jane cares for athletes while living her busy coaching life, so in the final section, some implications and questions are presented for consideration.

Introduction to Jane

Jane is in her 40s and is a practicing coach in endurance and long-distance running events. She has a wealth of experience including coaching athletes in universities, national teams, international camps and competitions. She works as a national selector (under 20s age group), as an individual coach to athletes (under 21s) and as a coach for a national governing body (under 18s, under 20s and seniors). Across these roles, Jane cares for athletes in a maternal manner that seems to be consistent with Noddings' (2005) approach to caring. As Jane describes it:

> At the last competition, I was the only female member of staff, and funnily enough, one of the coaches who has never been before said, "If they are emotionally upset, my suggestion is that you look after the girls, and I will look after the boys." I said, "I think you might find it the other way round." I do not know why, but there are a number of boys in that squad who will always come to me no matter what. I mean one of them was in tears after a bad race, he was really upset, and he broke down in tears with me. I am not sure he would have done that with a guy. I think there is a maternal element to it. That athlete has been in the squad for two years now. I have known them the whole way through since they were 15. I have had a bit of an impact on him, I think.

Biography

Jane was not always a coach. She worked as a teacher in a primary (elementary) school for 18 years, was an elite athlete and worked in sport business for a clothing company. As a primary school teacher, Jane invested long hours in planning and nurturing young people. The primary teacher role has long been associated with maternal care (Noddings, 2005), and in the UK female practitioners predominantly perform this role. Noddings' (2005) analysis of female-dominated professions such as primary school teaching recognised that these roles require practitioners to care through dialogue, empathy and nurturing individuals. Jane similarly recognises a link between primary education and care based on her career experience as a teacher, and furthers this link by connecting it directly to her coaching experiences:

> When you have taught 4- and 5-year-olds, and looked after their needs, and learnt how to calm them down when they are upset, and I have taught reception and nursery at one stage, and they have to leave the parents for the first time. This stands you in good stead when coaching teenagers.
>
> You are in loco parentis when you are coaching. You have a duty of care legally. When athletes have a bad race, their depression is sky high and if they have a good race, their depression is low. But even then, fatigue creeps in towards the end of the week and that is a challenge for them. They are knackered by the end of a European competition and you are responsible for them. Despite the fatigue, one particular parent said to me, "I want them to do every race they can. I don't want them to skip races for rest and if you want I will write a letter saying I will take responsibility." I said, "You can't legally do that, because it is me that is there, I have the duty of care, I have the responsibility. If she is getting tired or fatigued, I will take her out of the race to protect her. You can write a letter if you want, but at the end of the day it is on my head and I have to protect her."

While maternal like care is an essential aspect of Jane's coaching, she is also devoted to analytical work and achieving objectively defined outcomes – as might be expected of a former elite athlete in high-performance sport who competed in international events. Jane also found these skills were necessary to succeed in a post she held in sales and marketing at an international clothing company. That said, Jane feels that her work in that company was not always valued because, as a female, she was not considered to be 'management material':

> You know it's funny. As a teacher I used to think the world was completely equal because, you know, teaching is female dominated. I never saw a glass ceiling, and if anybody had mentioned it to me, I would have just ignored it and said, "Stop whinging." I did, however, find a glass ceiling in sales. That was my first experience of it and it is why I left really. It was why I went back into sport. I was doing quite a demanding and responsible job and I had to fight for the recognition of what I was doing. I had to fight more and more, and eventually I went to my boss for my review appraisal, and I made myself this A3-sized business card and listed all the responsibilities I had. I went in and said, "This is my new business card. That is my role. That is what I do." And he laughed and was great. He said, "You're right; you are doing all this stuff and not really getting the recognition for it."
>
> In sales, you see, the culture was a lot of men going to Arsenal (a premier league football club) for the game together and socialising. And then saying, "This is a good guy, get him in as a manager," rather than considering the females who were not at the game. And a lot of them (males) didn't see women as managers and never saw women in those roles. I mean, one boss actually said to me at one stage, "You will be going off and having babies at some stage." And I never did. I don't have children. His wife was very much the stay at home kind, and I just kind of looked at him and thought, "You just see me as the same as what you have got at home and I am not that person. I am much more ambitious career wise."

Thus, with both an appreciation of maternal care from teaching and a steely ambition to progress, Jane embarked on a coaching career. Helped by networks made as a former athlete and through her sport business contacts, Jane secured voluntary and paid sessional coaching opportunities alongside a paid full-time job as a sport development officer. In that role, she worked for a national governing body of sport and was tasked with developing performance systems, pathways, talent camps and athletes that would ultimately lead to success for junior athletes in international competition.

Context

At the time of our first interview, Jane was a busy coach. As a volunteer, she coached two athletes 'remotely.' This involved Skyping an athlete who was on scholarship at a university in the US and visiting an athlete who was based in another part of the country. Jane uses technology at home to analyse athlete performances and to plan training programmes for them. In addition, Jane coaches a university team three times a week. This is a voluntary, informal position that involves organising training facilities and times, planning programmes, informing students about competitions and developing a successful running group:

> I was asked to coach at the university by an athlete, so I was never approached by the university or applied for a job formally. An athlete who went there said, "We have not got a coach and would you be interested?" I was looking for coaching opportunities at the time, because I was on a national coach development programme which is a mentoring scheme. I had my two girls, but felt I needed a bit more coaching to benefit from the mentoring. So I went down for the first session and got there early to have a look at the area, to think where am I going to run this session and the athlete turned up and I said, "We are going to go on those fields over there." And he said, "Oh no we're not. We can't. We are not allowed." I said, "What do you mean we are not allowed? This is the university and you are not allowed on your own fields?" Eventually, the university found out that I was coaching, and they said to me, "Oh we are really happy that you are coaching the athletes, and can we make it a bit more official? We can't pay you, but we could support you with maybe expenses for going to competitions." I said, "Before you do that, I am not prepared to be recognised as the coach for this university until you find us somewhere safe to train," 'cause I was taking them out on the roads, and it was ridiculous. There followed lots and lots of meetings

and I identified these fields that are not the first team pitches, just back fields and they share them with the local school. I said, "Surely we can run around these? What is the problem?" They weren't happy, so I went to the school to see the caretaker, the grounds man there, and I said to him, "I am coaching at the university, we want to run round the fields that we share, what's your thoughts?" And he said, "Of course you can." So I then went back to the university and said, "Well, the school have given us permission" and the university reluctantly said, "Well if they have given you permission, I suppose we should give you permission as well cause we share." But they have never made it easy. They don't open the gates, so we have to climb through a hole in the fence. There is no lighting there, so I have to bring these led lights with me. It takes a lot of setting up.

Initial analysis by Colum Cronin

Many coaches reading this will recognise Jane's experience. For example, volunteerism is a key feature of the wider context of coaching in many sports in the UK, where 76% of coaches operate on a voluntary basis (Sports Coach UK, 2015). Additionally, like Jane, the majority of coaches practice in sports clubs or educational establishments (Sports Coach UK, 2015). Jane couples her voluntary work with paid roles for national governing bodies and again readers may have experiences of these contexts. Readers may also recognise that Jane's coaching is characterised as caring activity. This manifests itself in simple activities such as ensuring facilities for athletes are safe. Additionally, Jane's caring is evident in her relationships with athletes, which are based upon dialogue, empathy and a desire to serve their needs. These characteristics are consistent with Noddings' (2003) 'caring for' concept (previously discussed in Chapter 2). They are also consistent with Noddings' view of pedagogy as a relationship based upon care. Indeed, Jane's pedagogy is focused on helping athletes learn, grow and achieve both social and sporting outcomes. This notion of sport pedagogy is shared across much sport coaching including voluntary clubs, professional teams and publicly funded organisations (Armour, 2011). In that sense, regardless of context, coaching is essentially a pedagogical act (Cronin & Armour, 2017; Armour, 2011), and Jane could certainly be characterised as a 'pedagogue-coach.' Accordingly, the first disciplinary analysis will further consider Jane's care through Noddings' caring pedagogy theory. Jane's pedagogical relationships are, however, situated in wider social contexts that are influenced by political and economic factors. Therefore, the second disciplinary analysis will utilise sociology of education to consider how Jane cares in an elite sport context.

Theoretical perspective 1: Noddings' ethically informed pedagogy

Pedagogy is a term that is often used in academia to denote the study and practice of teaching and learning. Tinning (2008) defines pedagogy as a purposeful encounter between teachers and learners where practitioners seek to meet the needs of learners. More recently, Armour (2011; Armour & Chambers, 2014) have situated pedagogy within sport and exercise contexts by arguing that coaches, PE teachers and exercise professionals are essentially concerned with using multi and interdisciplinary knowledges to facilitate learning. In so doing, it is argued that teaching/coaching always involves a learner/athlete, and that pedagogical activity should be focused on the needs of those learners. Consistent with this insight, Noddings' (2005) pedagogical approach argues that learners should be at the heart of any pedagogical activity. From an ethical perspective, Noddings is clear that pedagogical practice needs to respect both the autonomy and beneficence of learners. Based upon this premise, Noddings (2005) argued that effective pedagogies occur within caring relationships because teachers (coaches) need to understand the needs of learners (engrossment) and act for the benefit of learners (motivational displacement). Specifically, pedagogical actions should be undertaken in direct response to the needs, actions and concerns of learners. Thus, from Noddings' ethical perspective, teachers can care about pupils, but they are only in caring relationships with the consent and benefit of learners.

Having worked with Jane in the construction of her narrative, it would appear that she is a coach whose pedagogy occurs within caring relationships. These relationships are formed for the benefit of athletes. As an example, Jane's concern for her athletes does not finish with the final whistle. Rather, off the field spaces such as hotels and transport provide opportunities where Jane nurtures her athletes with their beneficence in mind:

> I will bring chocolate milk to the finish line so the athletes can have it as soon as possible. To be honest, if they had a really bad race I (Jane) have to mop up tears, or sometimes they are *hyper* and I have to calm them down. They are either crying or laughing and I deal with that. I don't know why but there are a number of boys in that squad who will always come to me if they are emotionally upset. After I deal and comfort them, I have to get them back to the tent and get them recovered quite quickly. We will do the cool down as soon as we can and I run a bath for them at the hotel. If there is a pool, we get them swimming, and we see to all that kind of stuff for them. In the evening, we don't want them doing much so we get them to put their feet up and rest.
>
> (Cronin & Armour, 2017, P. 924)

In addition to nurturing athletes after races, Jane's maternal pedagogical approach extends to supervising her athletes at social events. Again, these acts are for the athletes' benefit:

> On Sunday night, I was out night clubbing with athletes until three o'clock in the morning. That is why I have a cold. I am not used to that. We were up at six to get the flight back to Manchester, but the last night at competition was planned as a social night out, so we went out. Even though it was a night out for me, I was also on duty. I was constantly watching the juniors to make sure they did not drink too much and to make sure they were on the bus to get back to the hotel. In that sense, I was socialising, but I was also working quite hard, and there was no way I would have drunk alcohol, because I had to look after the athletes.

These beneficent acts illustrate a devoted, caring, responsible and athlete-centred coach. Such practice is congruent with other examples of caring coaches that suggest caring may be a core feature of good coaching practice (e.g. Annerstedt & Eva-Carin, 2014; Jones, 2015; Jones, 2009; Knust & Fisher, 2015).

Consistent with Noddings' (2005) ethical pedagogical approach, Jane's caring is also based on dialogue that involves athletes accepting care. For example, prior to competitive events, Jane initiates dialogue to understand athletes' needs (engrossment) better:

> At youth European competitions, we attend technical meetings to get information for athletes. I give the athletes their individual start time because it is not a mass start and the athletes are in quarantine before they race. Quarantine is an area where athletes go to before the race, and they are not allowed to have any contact with the outside world. I make sure they know what bus they have to take to the quarantine, how long they are going to be there and what they need to take with them like books and music. I ask them, "How do you want the atmosphere to be in quarantine, do you want me to chat to you, do you want me to tell you some jokes, do you want it light hearted, do you want some time on your own."

Dialogue is an essential concept within Noddings' (2005) pedagogical approach, which ensures that care is enacted *with* rather than *upon* athletes. More specifically, Noddings argues that care should be informed, received and acknowledged by learners. It is argued that dialogue both empowers and tasks learners to play an active part in their relationships and learning. Indeed, Noddings (2005) goes so far as to state, "Without an affirmative response from the cared-for, we cannot call an encounter or relation, caring." In support of this argument, a range of pedagogical theorists (e.g. Dewey, 1916; Freire, 2005; Vygotsky, 1987; Wenger, 1998) have also stressed the importance of dialogue in learning. Noddings (2005) builds on this work by emphasising that communication should be authentic. Authentic dialogue involves genuinely listening to young people rather than attempting to gather consensus or elicit coercive agreement to a predetermined decision. Unfortunately, Noddings (2005, p. 53) laments, "There is little real dialogue in classrooms. A typical pattern of talk can be described this way: Teacher elicitation, student response, teacher evaluation."

Literature, which has examined the pedagogical activity of coaches, has also evidenced Noddings' concerns about communication that is inauthentic, controlled or dictated by coaches. Case studies of coaching reported by Cushion and Jones (2012); Potrac, Jones and Cushion

(2007); and Cushion and Jones (2006) provide examples of coaches who have tended to use questioning and dialogue in a manner that reinforces the coach's position of authority, rather than including athletes in ethical ways. It has been suggested that such action may be informed by coaches' attempts to retain power or engage in impression management (Partington & Cushion, 2012; Potrac et al., 2007; Potrac, Jones, & Armour, 2002). Despite these hypotheses, further work is needed to generalise more broadly from these case studies. Nonetheless, Jane's case suggests that authentic dialogue, based upon genuine listening and concern for the needs of athletes, may have much to offer in terms of establishing an ethical caring – rather than dictatorial relationship – between coaches and athletes. Specifically, in Jane's case, authentic dialogue, which often occurs off the field of play, is a precursor to understanding (engrossment) and acting upon the needs of learners (motivational displacement). Moreover, authentic communication wherein Jane *listens* to athletes' is a means by which athletes consent, receive and acknowledge Jane's caring pedagogy.

Theoretical perspective 2: Lynch's (feminist) sociology of education

Thus far, Jane has been portrayed as a caring coach who exhibits Noddings' (2005) key concepts of engrossment, motivational displacement, authentic dialogue and ethical caring relationships. Noddings' care theory has, however, been critiqued for failing to recognise that caring relationships are situated within wider social contexts that impinge upon them (Purdy, Potrac, & Paulauskas, 2016). It is important that the contexts in which caring occurs are examined critically to consider how social structures – e.g., cultures, institutions and practices – might influence caring. To that end, the work of Lynch (2010) is interesting. Although her work is focussed on developing a sociological understanding of caring in higher education institutions, there are clear parallels with contemporary coaching.

Grummell, Devine and Lynch (2009) uses the concept of 'new managerialism' to analyse higher education. This is a term that characterises managerial cultures where monitoring of staff performance through quantifiable performance indicators is prioritised. These quantifiable measurements are then used to regulate internal competition and thus create a competitive market between staff. For some time now, sociologists in the UK have noted how new managerial practices from the private sector have been adopted by institutions in the wider public sector. In the UK, it has been argued that government-funded sport has also adopted a new managerialist approach (Houlihan & Green, 2009). This is most evident in UK sport's no-compromise approach, where competitive success (i.e. medals) is linked directly to funding and employment status. Jane acknowledges that she operates in this kind of managerialist culture:

> In our sport, we get funding from a governing body who agrees targets with my line manager. My line manager is the performance and talent manager. She agrees our target, and she says what we think we can achieve and the governing body negotiate with her in terms of medals. Anyway, our target this year was to get six top-20 places at junior world championships. We were targeted to get six, but we actually got five. That was considered ok because the difference was not too drastic. If we only had two or three medals, then we would have had our funding cut.

Lynch (2010) makes the important point that while performance indicators are often quantifiable, they are far from neutral. Adopting a sociological imagination approach that questions hidden assumptions (Mills, 2000), Lynch argues that emotional labour such as caring is not often captured by quantifiable performance measures. Therefore, caring may not be valued in contexts that solely prioritise quantifiable accounts of performance. Thus, the internal competition between staff results in targets that are not neutral because the quantification process prioritises those aspects that can be 'objectively' measured. Nurturing and caring do not sit easily in this rubric.

Taking a critical view of new managerialism, Grummell et al. (2009) also introduced the notion of 'care *full*' workers. This describes those professionals whose working lives may involve lots of nurturing care (e.g. for students or athletes) and whose personal lives may also feature nurturing care (e.g. for children or elderly relatives). Grummell, Devine and Lynch contrasted these care full individuals with 'care *less*' individuals who are less actively engaged in the grounded work of caring. In the context of higher education institutions, Grummell et al. (2009, p. 197) noted how at "the higher levels; the academic career structures increasingly demand single-minded dedication to one's profession" and therefore senior positions are often filled by those unencumbered by caring – i.e., care less workers. Indeed, Lynch (2010, p. 63) argues that care less workers are best placed to succeed in a "24/7 culture of availability, and migratory and transnational lifestyles" that characterises new managerialist cultures. This is an issue that Jane has also noted in the competitive and new managerialist world of elite sport coaching:

> You know sport happens in the weekends and in the evenings. That is when people are free to train and compete. During the day, I am doing the logistical side of things. The athletes will ring me in the evening and on weekends. Parents will ring as well. The parents will often send me an email in the day saying, "Can you ring us tonight at seven o'clock." I cannot turn around and say, "No, I don't work at seven o'clock."

The impact of a competitive, demanding and 24/7 new managerialist culture can be seen in Jane's personal life. For example, Jane has limited social time with her wider family. This is because she invests much of her time in achieving coaching targets or caring for athletes:

> Before we went to Bulgaria this time, my dad actually said to me in quite a stern voice, "For god's sake, you are never in this country. You are always going somewhere." My family thinks I work too hard, and they do miss me. I am not around as much as they would like me to be, or as much as I would like to be as well. This week I got back on Monday from Bulgaria. Tuesday, I went to the office to pick up all the equipment for the training camp on Wednesday, because I could not get my head around that before I went to Bulgaria. After that, I rushed over to my parents on Tuesday night for dinner with my family, and I think my sister said, "Oh, what are you doing tomorrow." I said, "Oh, I am off to my next coaching camp." Sometimes, I do think I would like to have some time to see my friends and family more. I do not have much time to see people. I do not socialise outside of work much. Yeah, I do too much work.

Lynch (2010, p. 63) empathises with the demands placed upon workers such as Jane and argues that unfortunately care less working "has been endorsed as morally worthy" in cultures that reward "aggressive competitiveness and ruthlessness." Similarly, Jane suggests that in the senior levels of sport coaching, nurturing care may not be valued and that a cut-throat and cold leader is the type that is most likely to be rewarded:

> I think for my new job (performance director) they wanted somebody that was much more cut throat. More cold and detached . . . That actually isn't me, yet. But they couldn't afford that type of person, so I got it.

Consistent with Jane's experience, Lynch argues that in many organisations, there is a ceiling, above which care full individuals are unlikely to rise. This care ceiling prohibits individuals who have care full lives (professionally or personally) from achieving senior roles for two reasons: 1) caring skills are underappreciated in connection with senior roles and 2) the intense time demands of caring (for learners or family) prohibit individuals whose lives are 'care full' from succeeding in new managerialist cultures. Lynch's observations on higher education resonate with Jane's coaching experiences, which suggest individuals with caring skills may not be prioritised for high-level positions. Building on this notion further, and writing from a feminist perspective that critically considers the experiences of women, Lynch (2010) argues that 'care ceilings' are experienced disproportionately by female staff. This argument is made on the basis that women tend to engage in more caring work in their professional lives (e.g. nurturing athletes) and/or personal lives (e.g. caring for children).[1] As a result, women are more likely to live care full lives that are time consuming, yet underappreciated, which means they encounter a 'care ceiling' that prohibits their progression to senior roles. Jane describes this conundrum in action in vivid terms:

> Last week, there was a discussion session on the lack of women in sport at performance level, and what can we do about it? Many groups identified many reasons why. Family commitments came through as a strong one. We talked more about the recruitment process. I had to challenge one group. I could not quite believe

my ears! They said, "If a performance director position was advertised now, there would be very few women who had the knowledge and skills to be able to do it." I put my hand up and said, "Why are you saying that women haven't got the knowledge and skills to do that role? Is it a perception that, of what a performance director should look like, should be and should the leadership style that they should have? Because that is what it sounds like to me. I mean, I think there's lots of women out there who've got the knowledge and skills to do it, but they're not appointed, because people see leadership styles as male. They recognise more of a male leadership style, and they don't necessarily recognise a female leadership style." We could talk about this all day, but what I am saying is, "I'm not that cut throat person that they were talking about."

Jane's experiences suggest that a maternal nurturing form of care is essential, time consuming, yet undervalued at the highest levels of sport coaching. This view is consistent with the experiences of this author (Colum) who has also observed the "cut-throat" world of elite sport. Similarly, previous research on female coaching has identified a patriarchal social context in sport (LaVoi & Dutove, 2012; Norman, 2010a, 2010b). Moreover, elite coaching contexts have been characterised by authoritarianism, hierarchical deference, masculinity (Cushion & Jones, 2006) and conflict (Potrac & Jones, 2009; Potrac, Jones, Gilbourne, & Nelson, 2012; Thompson, Potrac, & Jones, 2013). Thus, from a sociological perspective, the new managerialist and competitive world of coaching that Jane inhabits seems to undervalue the development of caring, nurturing relationships. This conclusion has implications for coaches, coach educators, coach employers and coaching researchers because care is at the heart of pedagogical relationships.

Implications from Jane's story

Jane's story illustrates a paradox. From a pedagogical perspective, Jane's care is an essential aspect of her practice. She engages in nurturing acts that are informed by reciprocal dialogue, values listening, and delivers caring acts that occur beyond the field of play. Thus, caring within authentic dialogical relationships is part of Jane's essential and ethical coaching practice. She 'cares for' her athletes in a manner that Noddings (2005) would recognise. Simultaneously, Jane recognises a coaching culture which does not value care – one which is characterised by competitiveness and appears to value what she views as 'cold' and more detached leaders. Jane therefore faces a challenge of caring for athletes and her wider family in an environment that does not promote care. Coaches, coach developers, coach employers and coach researchers have much work to do in order to address the challenges within Jane's story and to ensure that caring takes a more central and valued role in effective coaching practice. Specifically:

1   We need to be certain as coaches that athletes have consented to our coaching. **Coaches** should consider, do we know our athletes well enough to be sure? What kinds of self-reflection, dialogue and listening skills are required to develop that level of knowing?

2   If knowing and involving athletes is an ethical precursor to helping them to flourish, what kinds of caring skills do coaches need and where could they develop them? **Coach educators** must support coaches to engage in caring relations including developing listening skills, supporting coaches whose lives are care full and recognising/'calling out' the existence of a potential care ceiling. How can this be achieved, and where will coach educators learn their skills?

3   A small but growing corpus of evidence suggests that caring relationships may be a precursor to excellent coaching. It would be appropriate, therefore, for **coach employers** such as National Governing Bodies (NGBs) and professional teams to reconsider the role and value of care in coaching to ensure they are not missing something in their current practices. Explicitly acknowledging the role of care may lead to a reimagining of new managerialist culture, which, in turn, could lead to more inclusive coaching cultures for those coaches who live care full lives.

4   Females are underrepresented in sport coaching, and yet a care ceiling may have a disproportional negative impact on females. So how can sports ensure that female coaches are supported?

5   **Coach researchers** have a duty to work collaboratively in the cultures of elite sport coaching to critically name and review established coaching practices, particularly the belief that new managerialist processes are objective, neutral and unproblematic.

Researchers should consider; What are the experiences of 'care full' coaches; how are athletes who require care cared for – and by whom?

In summary, Jane's story suggests that all stakeholders in coaching need to work together to understand better how ethical and caring coaching can flourish in ways that enhance the experiences of athletes.

Note

1 See Chapter 2 and the work of Gilligan (1982) and Noddings (2003) for further discussion on the gendered notion of care.

Bibliography

Annerstedt, C., & Eva-Carin, L. (2014). Caring as an important foundation in coaching for social sustainability: A case study of a successful Swedish coach in high-performance sport. *Reflective Practice, 15*(1), 27–39. doi:10. 1080/14623943.2013.869204

Armour, K. M. (2011). *Sport pedagogy: An introduction for teaching and coaching* (1st ed.). London: Routledge.

Armour, K. M., & Chambers, F. C. (2014). 'Sport & exercise pedagogy': The case for a new integrative sub-discipline in the field of Sport & Exercise Sciences/Kinesiology/Human Movement Sciences. *Sport, Education and Society, 19*(7), 855–868. doi:10.1080/13573322.2013.859132

Cronin, C., & Armour, K. M. (2017). 'Being' in the coaching world: New insights on youth performance coaching from an interpretative phenomenological approach. *Sport, Education and Society, 22*(8), 919–931. doi: 10.1080/13573322.2015.1108912

Cushion, C., & Jones, R. L. (2006). Power, discourse and symbolic violence in professional youth soccer: The case of Albion FC. *Sociology of Sport Journal, 23*(2), 142–161. doi:10.1123/ssj.23.2.142

Cushion, C., & Jones, R. L. (2012). A Bourdieusian analysis of cultural reproduction: Socialisation and the 'hidden curriculum' in professional football. *Sport, Education and Society, 19*(3), 1–23. doi:10.1080/13573 322.2012.666966

Dewey, J. (1916/2011). *Democracy and education*. Los Angeles: Simon and Brown.

Freire, P. (2005). *Pedagogy of the oppressed* (4 ed.). (M. Bergman Ramos, Trans.). New York, NY: Continuum.

Gilligan, C. (1982). *In a different voice*. Boston, MA: Harvard.

Grummell, B., Devine, D., & Lynch, K. (2009). The care-less manager: Gender, care and new managerialism in higher education. *Gender and Education, 21*(2), 191–208. doi:10.1080/09540250802392273

Houlihan, B., & Green, M. (2009). Modernization and sport: The reform of sport England and UK sport. *Public Administration, 87*(3), 678–698. doi:10.1111/j.1467-9299.2008.01733.x

Jones, C. (2015). Care and phronesis in teaching and coaching: Dealing with personality. *Sport, Education and Society.* doi:10.1080/13573322.2015.1015976

Jones, R. L. (2009). Coaching as caring (the smiling gallery): Accessing hidden knowledge. *Physical Education and Sport Pedagogy, 14*(4), 377–390. doi:10.1080/17408980801976551

Knust, S. K., & Fisher, L. A. (2015). NCAA division I female head coaches' experiences of exemplary care within coaching. *International Sport Coaching Journal, 2*(2), 94–107. doi:10.1123/iscj.2013-0045

LaVoi, N. M., & Dutove, J. K. (2012). Barriers and supports for female coaches: An ecological model. *Sports Coaching Review, 1*(1), 17–37. doi:10.1080/21640629.2012.695891

Lynch, K. (2010). Carelessness: A hidden doxa of higher education. *Arts and Humanities in Higher Education, 9*(1), 54–67. doi:10.1177/14740 22209350104

Mills, C. W. (2000). *The sociological imagination.* Oxford: Oxford University Press.

Noddings, N. (2003). *Caring: A feminine approach to ethics and moral education.* Berkeley, CA: University of California Press.

Noddings, N. (2005). *The challenge to care in schools: An alternative approach to education* (2nd ed.). New York, NY: Teachers College Press.

Norman, L. (2010a). Feeling second best: Elite women coaches' experiences. *Sociology of Sport Journal, 27*(1), 89–104. doi:10.1123/ssj.27.1.89

Norman, L. (2010b). Bearing the burden of doubt: Female coaches' experiences. *Research Quarterly for Exercise and Sport, 81*(4), 506–517. doi:10.1080/02701367.2010.10599712

Partington, M., & Cushion, C. J. (2012). Performance during performance: Using Goffman to understand the behaviours of elite youth football coaches during games. *Sports Coaching Review, 1*(2), 93–105. doi:10.1080/21640629.2013.790167

Potrac, P., & Jones, R. L. (2009). Micropolitical workings in semi-professional football. *Sociology of Sport Journal, 26*(4), 557–577. doi:10.1123/ssj.26.4.557

Potrac, P., Jones, R. L., & Armour, K. (2002). It's all about getting respect': The coaching behaviors of an English soccer coach. *Sport, Education and Society, 7*(2), 183–202. doi:10.1080/1357332022000018869

Potrac, P., Jones, R. L., & Cushion, C. (2007). Understanding power and the coach's role in professional English soccer: A preliminary investigation of coach behaviour. *Soccer & Society*, *8*(1), 33–49. doi:10.1080/14660970600989509

Potrac, P., Jones, R. L., Gilbourne, D., & Nelson, L. (2012). 'Handshakes, BBQs, and bullets': Self-interest, shame and regret in football coaching. *Sports Coaching Review*, *1*(2), 79–82. doi:10.1080/21640629.2013.768418

Purdy, L., Potrac, P., & Paulauskas, R. T. (2016). Nel Noddings. In L. Nelson, R. Groom, & P. Potrac (Eds.), *Learning in sports coaching: Theory and application* (pp. 215–227). Oxon: Routledge.

Sports Coach UK. (2015). *The coaching panel 2015: A report on coaches and coaching in the UK*. Leeds: Sports Coach UK.

Thompson, A., Potrac, P., & Jones, R. (2013). 'I found out the hard way': Micropolitical workings in professional football. *Sport, Education and Society*. doi:10.1080/13573322.2013.862786

Tinning, R. (2008). Pedagogy, sport pedagogy, and the field of kinesiology. *Quest*, *60*(3), 405–424. doi:10.1080/00336297.2008.10483589

Vygotsky, L. (1987). Thought and language. In A. Kozulin (Ed.), *Thought and language*. Cambridge, MA: MIT Press.

Wenger, E. (1998). *Communities of practice*. New York, NY: Cambridge University Press.

5 Caring through science and autonomy

Terry's story

Colum Cronin, Kathleen Armour and Kevin Enright

This chapter presents Terry's story. Terry's story builds on the previous chapters by 1) illustrating how technology and science can be useful mechanisms to facilitate care and 2) by considering the apparently contradictory notions of care and athlete autonomy. The chapter begins by introducing Terry, his background and the context in which he coaches. Terry's story is then presented in his own words (using indented text). The story is structured and narrated around two themes: *developing a pedagogical relationship* and *using technology and science to care*. Following Terry's story, Colum Cronin offers an initial analysis. This is followed by two further analyses. Firstly, Colum further explores the ways in which Terry's pedagogical practice balances athlete autonomy and care. Following Colum's analysis, Kevin Enright discusses the role of the sport scientist in caring for athletes. Kevin provides a practitioner perspective that draws upon his own experience as a sport scientist in top-flight English Football (soccer). He considers how data can be both an enabler and barrier to developing and maintaining caring relationships. Both of these analyses add new dimensions to Noddings' (2005) established view of care. The chapter concludes with a summary of take-home messages.

Introduction to Terry

Now in his 70s, Terry runs regularly and is often seen in his tracksuit in the city centre. At Starbucks, where I (Colum) meet him, everybody knows Terry. He is a character, but he does not describe himself as such. Rather, he declares that he is an "old school, classically educated" coach. This description refers to Terry's training at a PE college, years of practice as a physical educator and drama teacher in secondary (high) schools and a long and decorated career as an athletics coach. Terry has now retired from teaching, but he still works as a coach mentor for a national governing body. Alongside this role and his previous role as a teacher, Terry also coaches athletes (14 years upwards) in sprint events. Some of Terry's athletes have performed and won medals at the highest levels of international competition, including the Olympic Games. Even today, Terry has athletes participating in major international events, for example, the European Championships.

Terry may have retired from PE teaching, but in terms of coaching, educating and athletics, he is a 'lifer.' This is easy to recognise from the way in which he describes himself, his philosophy and his practice. It is also obvious that Terry cares for young people's development. He has high expectations, tolerates 'no nonsense' and challenges athletes to grow. He is passionate about his sport (athletics) and passionate about learning. As a former PE teacher, Terry is also one of those coaches who believes in covering more than a curriculum in order to give 'life lessons' through sport. I imagine Terry would get you fit for a race. At the same time, I believe Terry would take every opportunity to offer timely nuggets of advice such as remembering to "shake hands firmly" in order to make good impression at a job interview. In many ways, Terry is the personification of that philosophy of coaching, which is underpinned by the belief that coaching is about educating individuals for challenges to come:

> You educate athletes to independently cope and bring them up in a way so that they can do without the coach. Having said that, an athlete occasionally needs a pair of eyes to watch, or a sounding board. But to perform extremely well, an athlete has to understand what they do and why they do it. The athlete has to be in control of what they do, and I say to athletes, "It is your responsibility, you have to develop, take ownership, and evaluate. And I have to educate."
>
> In the beginning, you are in more of a teacher pupil relationship, and then once the athletes reach that sort of late teens age, the parents don't come down quite so often to watch the athletes train. They do not see the transition in relationship, but athletes that start young with me are brought up to know and appreciate their own knowledge.
>
> My role as a coach is to educate, to bring the athlete to a stage where they no longer need me. I constantly encourage a dialogue,

and I am constantly encouraging the athlete to understand why we do what we do. I tell the athletes, "I have to justify everything to you. Ask me! If I can't justify it, then don't do it."

Biography

Terry came into coaching in his early 20s as a result of frustration with his own coach. Terry recognised that his coach was both a good coach and a good person, but that he lacked the requisite technical knowledge for Terry's specific individual event. In response, Terry began self-coaching by planning his own sessions and evaluating his performances, yet he recognised that if he was going to improve, he needed other athletes around to challenge him. His solution was to include and coach a small group of athletes in his personal training sessions. One day, when Terry was in his late 20s, one of these athletes beat Terry in a national championship final. At that point, Terry realised that he might be a better coach than an athlete! This was a turning point, and Terry focused on coaching from that point forward.

In addition to his coaching experiences, Terry also trained at a PE teaching college in "the good old days" when PE courses were very practical. He credits this training with providing great technical knowledge, and he believes that his years spent teaching PE and drama honed his pedagogical knowledge, developed the skills of reflective practice and informed his 'coaches' eye':

> I can honestly say being a PE teacher is a big advantage. When I was a PE teacher, I planned every day. I looked at people perform right in front of my eyes. I developed a coach's eye. I reflected on how well they are doing as they were doing it. I had five lessons a day. There were five coaching sessions a day where I honed my art as a person that gives instructions based upon what I saw. It is an advantage to be a PE teacher because you are honing your art five times a day before you do a coaching session in the evening.

Context

When coaching, Terry places great importance on building one-to-one relationships and athlete-centred approaches. At the same time, Terry recognises that much can be gained from having a vibrant training group; so each year he works with a small group (6–16) of athletes on the track, in the gym and off the track. The athletes are of a good standard, and they have ambitions for success at national and international levels. These athletes range in age from 14 through to adult performers and include both male and female competitors. This means that Terry's athletes are often on different competitive programmes, and Terry has to find ways to work with the group as a whole, while also considering the needs of individual athletes.

All of Terry's athletes exist within what Côté and Gilbert (2009) define as the performance domain of sport. The performance domain is characterised by an "intensive commitment to a preparation programme for competition and a planned attempt to influence performance variables" (Côte & Gilbert, 2009, p. 314). Performance coaches such as Terry spend substantial amounts of time with athletes (Fraser-Thomas & Côté, 2009) and have specific training and performance goals in mind (Côté et al., 2007). For a small number of athletes within the group, Terry also works with their managers, medical staff and national governing body performance programmes. These athletes have reached the highest international levels

Terry has been a volunteer coach throughout his coaching career; for example, he worked as a teacher on weekdays while spending evenings and weekends coaching. This is typical of coaching athletics in the UK where full-time coaching positions have not been the norm. This is not to say that Terry is anything other than wholly 'professional'; rather, it simply means that he is not paid for coaching (Taylor & Garratt, 2010). Similarly, Terry's voluntary status does not mean he is not committed to athletes. On the contrary, Terry takes a long-term view of coaching and is willing to commit to an athlete for their entire career:

> I have to be careful who I take on as a coach, because it is not for a year or two; it is for 10 or 20 years. I have to be really careful. I have taken on two more athletes in September. It was a tough decision. Will I be around in ten years? One of the athletes was a more straightforward decision because that athlete is fairly mature anyway and probably only has three years left in his career. But the other athlete is younger, and it's ok, but I do wonder, "Will I still be around for her?" To be honest, I will

probably be coaching in some form until I die. I would think that I would carry on until I die really.

Terry's caring relationships

When I (Colum) began interviewing Terry, it was immediately obvious that he was an educator. Perhaps influenced by his teaching background, Terry emphasised learning, explanation and development during our interviews. Terry does not profess a didactic or one-way form of communication. On the contrary, he argues for a mature pedagogical relationship, where participants have a voice and are not helpless:

> You have to spend the time and explain to the athlete exactly why they are doing what they are doing. Once they understand that, then I think they buy into it better, and it just enables you to stand back a little bit and let them make decisions. It means they are far more empowered when they go out and compete. It also means you do not have to be there on competition day. They should be self-sufficient to be able to go to a competition, warm up and compete on their own. Athletes should not keep looking to the stands for reinforcement from the coach. It annoys me so intensely. It is particularly obvious with field eventers. As soon as the athlete has landed in the jumping pit, or has released the throwing implement, their eyes dart to the stands to see the coach to find out what happened. I think, well, you should think about that jump, reflect on it and know what happened without your coach.
>
> One of the truisms of coaching is that the athlete cannot see what the coach can, and the coach cannot feel what the athlete can. You see, I've never run anywhere the kind of speed that my athletes do. There is a difference in the feel and the way in which you distribute your speed when you run 47 seconds for a 400, compared with 44 seconds for a 400. This means that coaches will often use the language of the eye, but athletes will use language of feelings and should be able to interpret their feelings. Over the course of the season, I gradually change my language to respond to this. At the start, when I am in a teaching mode, it will be based upon what I see. By the end, it will be about how they feel. This is important, because if there is disconnect between the athlete and coach,

it is often because language is too visual and not about feeling and reflections. I encourage reflection from the athlete because then they teach you how they feel and that just empowers you to be a better coach for future generations.

Terry's emphasis on dialogue, listening to athletes and involving them in pedagogical decisions is consistent with Noddings' (2005) nurturing relationships as discussed in Chapter 2 and Chapter 4 (Jane's Story). In fact, over time, Terry establishes a working relationship where athletes are empowered to care for themselves:

> It is a challenge when you have athletes that transition to you when they are mature. I have somebody that's just come to me. He is in the twilight of his career. His previous coaches have been more trainers, rather than coaches. No that is probably not accurate. He has had someone that's been a coach/trainer as opposed to a coach/educator. Working with me has been quite a change for this athlete. Whenever I've asked for reflection from him, he's found it quite hard. He's never been asked to reflect before. But gradually, the athlete has learned how to reflect and to feedback, and I always encourage a response. For example, "Okay, do you need a rest? How tired are you? Do you want to stop there?"
>
> The idea of this athlete deciding not to complete what was set from the outset was a massive culture shock to him. He's always been told that working hard equals success and that working even harder equals even more success. Whereas at his age now, you've got to work smart, and you've got to take into account that you can't do the same volume and intensity of work that you did when you were 24. He has had many issues about feeling guilty when he did not complete what was set for the session. He always said, "Well you're the coach. What should I do? Should I do more?" I threw it back at him, and I said, "Yeah well you're the athlete, you decide." There's only one person in that partnership that fully understands and appreciates the impact that that training is having upon the body, and it's not the coach.
>
> Last week, we were doing a session, and it was a recovery session, therefore the volume of the work was not important. The purpose of the session is to feel a lot better at the end of it than

you did at the start. If you work too hard in the recovery session, it is going to impact upon your ability to do the important session the following day. We planned to do five runs, and after three runs, the same athlete said, "I think that's enough for me today." I slapped this athlete on the back and said, "Wow, you've come a long way in a short period of time." The athlete felt good about himself because he had made a good judgement call without depending on me.

Terry clearly values the views of athletes and encourages them to take responsibility for their care. It is important to be cautious here, because Terry has taken a long time to develop this level of autonomy amongst athletes. In fact, during our interviews, he was at pains to stress how his relationships develop over time from when athletes are young (e.g. 14 years old) to older athletes (e.g. 32 years old):

My journey as a coach is, initially a teacher, and they are a student. Then I become a coach, and they are an athlete. Then I become a mentor. I suppose in the end they mentor me back, and I love that. I love learning from them.

Caring through technology and science

Across the career of an athlete, Terry 'scaffolds' progressions and the autonomy of his athletes (Jones & Thomas, 2015). At times, and particularly with young athletes, Terry will make decisions in the best interests of the athlete. To help him care for athletes, Terry utilises technology to monitor training loads and recovery:

I have this mechanism to check and test them. It cost me a lot of money to buy it, and it is no bigger than a phone. The athletes do counter-movement jumps with it on. They do five of them in the warm up, and it tells me their force, velocity and power. It's brilliant because it is coach friendly. There are a couple of athletes that are more sensitive, and I know that if they reach certain scores, well if they can only reach certain scores then two or three days later they are likely going to be ill. So, they are like my barometer. On Monday when I tested them, a couple of them were near too near the knuckle. So, I just made yesterday a less intense day to stop them being ill. I had to justify myself yesterday, because I changed the programme. The guys turned up expecting something intense, and I changed it. Three out of the four athletes were very happy. The fourth said, "Hmmm, I am not sure. You are the coach but why are you changing it?" I reduced the volume and intensity of the work, because at the end of last week, the athletes were way too battered and too tired. I said, "Look, if we do the same volume and intensity this week as we did last week, some of you are going to get injured or more likely ill."

Thus, at times, Terry will use scientific measurements to care for athletes' health. He does this for the beneficence of athletes, which is consistent with Noddings' (2013) motivational displacement discussed previously (see Chapter 2). On such occasions, he combines these decisions with explanations. In that sense, Terry couples scientific practice with dialogue. Furthermore, as athletes' progress, Terry encourages athletes to take more ownership of their care. In doing so, Terry combines a caring approach with respect for the autonomy of individuals. Thus although the caring relationships and technology were presented under separate sub-headings, they are interlinked.

Initial analysis by Colum Cronin: two areas to contemplate

Terry's story raises at least two areas that are worthy of further analysis. Firstly, Terry's story is focused on his use of logical planning, scientific monitoring and mathematically determined work–rest ratios to care for athletes. This scientific approach to care is different to the maternal servitude associated with Noddings (2005). Indeed, Noddings' nurturing and empathising perspective was influenced by the work of Gilligan (1982) who wrote from a feminist perspective that was critical of scientific practices. Specifically, Gilligan regarded scientifically informed judgements as a blunt form of rule-based control that does not appreciate the perspectives of individuals. From this position, she argued that rule-based decision making and rigid scientifically informed actions can appear impersonal and may not consider the emotions of individuals.

A small corpus of recent coaching literature has also lent support to this argument. Specifically, Williams and Manley (2016) and Cronin, Whitehead, Webster and Huntley (2017) have highlighted the potential for sport science and technology to dehumanise athletes by reducing athletic experiences to quantifiable and universal measurements. These case studies have illustrated that coaches may see athletes as resources to be developed as part of an input and output process. This is far from the nurturing caring relationships that Noddings (2005) advocates. That said, Terry's story suggests that technology may not always dehumanise athletes. On the contrary, Terry's technology, measurements and rule-based judgements appear to have prompted further discussion with the athlete and ensured that the athlete remained healthy. Indeed, this appears to lead to greater understanding by the athletes. Thus, Terry's story prompts us to consider whether science and technology can enable or conversely limit care in coaching contexts. On a related theme, Reid, Buszard and Farrow (2018) recently suggested that coaches could manipulate playing field sizes and equipment ratios to prevent injuries and ensure appropriate training loads. The authors suggest that a critical consideration of sport science as a means of caring for the health of athletes is warranted. To explore this concept further, in the next section, Kevin Enright will draw upon his experiences as a sport scientist to further consider Terry's story.

In addition, to Kevin's analysis, Terry's story also prompts me (Colum) to consider the relationship between care and autonomy supporting coaching. Specifically, Terry recognises that athletes have knowledge and experiences that he will never have. He is aware that these knowledges bring value to him and the coaching relationship in general. With this premise in mind, Terry advocates a questioning and dialogical approach to coaching which respects the views and autonomy of the athlete. This is evident in the incidents noted earlier, where Terry encourages that athlete to decide when they have done enough training. When the athlete does make the decision, Terry respects the athlete's autonomy, understands that the athlete is well placed to appreciate his own body and praises him for making an autonomous decision. Of course, on another occasion the athlete may not have made the correct decision. In such an instance, offering such autonomy could be regarded as the antithesis of care and perhaps may lead to an injured athlete. Thus, in some circumstances, care and autonomy may not be harmonious concepts (Cronin et al., 2018). With this tension in mind, I further analyse the relationship between care and autonomy in a later section.

Theoretical perspective 1: a sport science analysis by Kevin Enright. Does sport science help or hinder caring?

Sports and exercise science incorporates a range of sub-disciplines that include physiology, psychology, biomechanics, nutrition, performance analysis and strength and conditioning. In professional sport, one of the main aims of the sports scientist is to work closely with the athlete, the coach and other colleagues to improve performance. Depending on the sport and the internal structures within the organisation, the sports scientist will have a range of roles that typically include collecting data to inform future decision-making processes. In my own (Kevin) physiology practice, I have gathered data that ranges from the number of hours the athlete sleep, the athlete's heart rate during training, to a urine or blood sample. This information can be actioned immediately or stored and later analysed with the fundamental intention to help coaches alter training programmes so as to achieve predefined training goals. Thus, 'sports scientists' are expected to be objective, methodical and 'evidenced based.' From this position, the role is not often explicitly associated with nurturing care.[1] That said, many sports scientists are implicitly involved in activities that can be directly linked to 'caring' for the athletes' health and well-being. The strength coach who rehabilitated the athlete from a broken leg, the nutritionist who screened the athlete for vitamin deficiencies or the physiologist who noticed an athletes body weight is dramatically dropping, are all examples of how the sports scientist can care for athletes through systematic, evidence-based practice. Thus, in some ways, caring as Terry does has much in common with sport science.

Upon reading Terry's story, I was intrigued to note that Terry commits to each athlete for 10 to 20 years. During this time, Terry is not only concerned about talent but also plays a caring role that contributes to the development of young people into adulthood. His holistic methods, and the relationships he builds, empower the athlete to make their own decisions. He challenges each person constantly to think for himself or herself and thus allows them to take ownership of the process. He hopes that 'one day' "they won't need him". In the world of modern professional sports (particularly team sports), it is rare that a sport scientist will work with an athlete for such an extended period across the athlete's career. For example, in some sports, there can be up to 20 support staff around a team of up to 40 athletes. In this regard, there can be many different interactions between athletes and staff every day, limiting the amount of time available to develop meaningful relationships. Thus, for many sports scientists caring acts are limited to short-term observations or interventions.

Terry's story has reminded me (Kevin) how data can be used to care for athletes. For example, Terry discusses how his data can predict if an athlete will get ill. Whilst the use of this type of methodology to predict illness is somewhat debatable (Jones et al., 2017), this simplified, human approach might be considered more effective than that of more complex interventions. This is because, Terry has the opportunity to contextualise any data collected with all of the other information he has encountered when interacting with the athlete, including feedback from the athlete following the last few training sessions, the splits from the sessions, having a deep understanding of the athletes' personality and lifestyle and, of course, his 'coaches eye.' In other performance environments, there can be lots of isolated 'data points', less 'human interaction' and more variables to consider. As a result, it is sometimes difficult for sport scientists to make clear recommendations or to have a real impact on the care of athletes. In my experience as a 'sports scientist' I have noticed that some of the data collection procedures create a situation that treats each athlete (Kennedy & Kennedy, 2016) as a number, or a piece of data that needs to be 'processed', rather than a human that needs care. Indeed, Kennedy and Kennedy (2016) note that modern football clubs' investment strategies promote sports science to be used to nurture young talent as a future asset rather than as a caring mechanism. Others also note that an over reliance on technology and data in modern coaching (Williams & Manley, 2016) can reduce the coaching process into a mundane exercise, the sole purpose of which is to develop players as commodities.

This 'mundane', 'data (ec)centric' approach is in line with some of my own experiences. I remember in a previous role as a 'sports scientist', I travelled with an international team of under-16 players to a tournament in Europe for about 10 days. Before I left, I was given a brief from my line manager to collect what he referred to as 'wellness data' every morning. Here, the intention was that this information could be used as a discussion point with the coach at breakfast and would inform how the players were 'cared for' during the day. Whilst in principle this was a logical idea, in practice, the situation became a laptop data entering process with little to no impact on the coaches' behaviour or the ability of the support staff to care for the athlete and/or help them achieve their goals. I recall it as follows:

> "Morning lads (the players), ok, could I (Kevin) just get you to take of your shoes and jump on the scales. Thanks, ok now the urine tube I gave you last night, did you remember to pee into it this morning? Great, just let me analyse this quickly. Whilst I'm doing this, can you pop some numbers into the laptop under your name, please. You just need to fill in how many hours you slept last night, the quality of your sleep, a score out of ten saying how fatigued you feel, a score to tell us how sore you are; if you are sore just pop in the box the muscles that are sore. Oh yea, can you fill in a score for your general health too, that would be great. Sorry, when you're done, the physio would like to test your hamstring flexibility and the strength of your adductors." Just 21 players to go! We will be at breakfast in no time!

After all the information was inputted into the laptop, I had ten minutes to decipher whether there were any care issues before the coaches met at breakfast. I arrived at breakfast with my laptop and was ready to inform the coaches' practice. I could describe the scenario as follows:

> "Hey coach, I (Kevin) just wanted to let you know that Johnny didn't recover well from training (he had nine out of ten on his fatigue score), and Mark didn't sleep that well last night (he had a two out of ten on his sleep quality score), so you might want to go easy on them today in training." He (the coach) looked at me like I'd just arrived off the latest ship from Mars, and said, "Yes, thanks, Kev. That's great, but I need Johnny and Mark to be involved today. We need to go through the high pressing phase of play that we have been working on. Oh, and there's a few other areas we need to work on, so we will need to see how they react when we get out there." I replied saying, "Ok, great, no problem, you're the boss. I will see you out at the field. I've just got to go and get all the GPS units and heart-rate belts ready." It was

at that point that I realised the goal was limited to gathering the data itself, rather than to use the data to care for players.

Whilst not universal, a mentality that sees players as "cogs in a performance machine" rather than as humans is too common in professional sport (Williams & Manley, 2016). Both my own experiences and the discussions I have had with other sports scientists corroborate this feeling. I believe this type of interaction can dehumanise the relationships between athletes, coaches and support staff, ultimately limiting any care that sports science or technology could provide. Thus, I was pleased and interested to see how Terry used technology to care. Specifically, Terry used technology within well-developed relationships that not only value the athletes as individuals but also involved athletes as part of the decision-making process. From this position, technology was used as a means to an end (i.e. caring for athletes), rather than as an end in itself (i.e. to produce an output or spreadsheet).

Theoretical perspective 2: a pedagogical analysis by Colum Cronin. Is care compatible with facilitating autonomy?

When reading Terry's story, it was obvious to me that Terry's pedagogical practice is aimed toward facilitating and developing athlete autonomy:

> I see myself as an educator. Educating those athletes on how we do it and why we do it. The training of PE teachers is not as good now as it used to be for decades. Which is a shame, because the greatest coaches in sport have always had a teacher training background.
>
> They should be self-sufficient to be able to go to a competition, warm up and compete on their own. Athletes should not keep looking to the stands for reinforcement from the coach. It annoys me so intensely.

Such a pedagogical approach is not new to sport coaching. Classic sport pedagogy literature such as Mosston's Styles (1966) and Bunker and Thorpe's (1982) Teaching Games for Understanding have advocated questioning as a means of initiating cognitive work that leads to athlete understanding and independent learning. Similarly, much sport psychology (e.g. Mageau & Vallerand, 2003; Deci & Ryan, 1985; Duda, 2013; Langdon, Harris, Burdette, & Rothberger, 2015) and more recent pedagogy literature (e.g. Nelson, Cushion, Potrac, & Groom, 2014; Kidman & Lombardo, 2010) have also argued for athletes and participants to take ownership of their learning. Despite this body of work, evidence suggests that much coaching practice remains coach centred and autocratic, with the voice of athletes rarely heard (Denison, Mills, & Konoval, 2017). For example, there is evidence that it is coaches who predominantly ask questions in training environments, and they do so in a didactic and closed manner that reinforces their own positions as gatekeepers of knowledge (Cope, Partington, Cushion, & Harvey, 2016). Against this backdrop, it is noteworthy that Terry encourages his athletes to question him and to exercise autonomous decision making about their own care:

> There's only one person in that partnership that fully understands and appreciates the impact that that training is having upon the body, and it's not the coach.

This role reversal demonstrates a respect for the autonomy of the individual and Terry's desire to listen to athletes rather than to elicit coercive agreement for a pre-determined decision. Answering athlete questions, listening to athlete's views and initiating conversations that are genuinely dialogic align with Noddings' (2005) care ethic. Specifically, as discussed in Chapter 2, Noddings argues that individuals need to receive, accept and acknowledge care autonomously in order for a relationship to be deemed consensual and caring.

Care and autonomy are, however, complex concepts. For example, through his emphasis on athlete autonomy, Terry could be seen as an absentee coach who neglected his duty to *care for* his athletes. There are two episodes that relate to this perspective. First, in his introduction, Terry explains passionately how he wants athletes to warm up on their own and reflect on their own performance. Secondly, in a later incident, Terry refuses to tell an athlete what to do; instead, he asks the athlete to make decisions about his own training load. Such actions could have negative consequences for the athlete's performance and health – e.g., injury could occur if the athlete does not warm up correctly. Yet, despite these potential consequences, Terry accedes to the view of the athlete in the decision-making process. An observer could perceive this as a neglectful act consistent with the absence of care. These incidents, therefore, prompted me to consider whether facilitating athlete autonomy is contradictory to care, or whether Terry could be caring about the long-term personal growth of his athlete by 'standing aside' and not intervening?

Upon first consideration, Terry's standing aside approach appears to be contradictory to Noddings' (2005) notions of a total engrossment and devoted maternal servitude. On secondary consideration, I tentatively suspect that standing aside is an act that Terry carefully considers. I reach this conclusion because Terry scaffolds his pedagogical approach throughout his athlete's career:

> You educate athletes to independently cope and bring them up in a way so that they can do without the coach . . . . I say to athletes, "It is your responsibility; you have to develop, take ownership and evaluate. And I have to educate."
>
> My journey as a coach is, initially a teacher, and they are a student. Then I become a coach, and they are an athlete. Then I become a mentor.

Thus, for me (Colum), Terry's standing aside is not neglect, but a means of caring for the long-term development of athletes through absence and challenge. Indeed, Terry has carefully scaffolded his practice to ensure that athletes are prepared for "the loneliness of competition." Additionally, Fine and Glendinning (2005, p. 616) support Terry's approach by arguing that it is important to respect the autonomy of both the carer and the cared for:

> Rather than being a unidirectional activity in which an active caregiver does something to a passive and dependent recipient . . . care is best understood as the product or outcome of the relationship between two or more people.

On this basis, if Terry were to deny the autonomy of athletes, he could be accused of engaging in smothering paternalism (Hargreaves & Tucker, 1991), or controlling behaviours that negatively influence athletes (Hedge & MacKenzie, 2012; Tomkins & Simpson, 2015). These outcomes are far from the reciprocal caring relationships based upon dialogue that Noddings advocates (see Chapter 2 for more discussion of Noddings' work). Caring therefore can involve a delicate balance of aiding individuals, whilst simultaneously respecting and facilitating the autonomy of individuals. Without an appropriate balance, individuals can be disempowered (too much intervention) or neglected (too little intervention). Terry strikes this balance by being empathetic to and meeting athlete's needs, whilst also providing space and time for personal growth and autonomy. Of course, this balance is influenced by situated factors – e.g., the experience of athletes. Terry's two-way dialogical relationship and his long-term 'scaffolded' pedagogy, therefore, appear to be a good example of a symbiotic and dynamic relationship, which changes over time but ensures that athletes are cared for as autonomous individuals.

Implications from Terry's story

Terry's story illustrates a long-term pedagogical approach to coaching, which is based upon care. Indeed, Terry makes a commitment to athletes and seeks to care for them across their careers. He does this by recognising that care is done *with*, rather than *to*, athletes. This caring practice is characterised by dialogue and athlete autonomy. It does, however, take time to develop these relationships, and Terry 'scaffolds' his relationships with athletes. As athletes develop, he facilitates more input and ownership from them. He also changes his language from a coach-led 'what he sees' approach to an athlete-centred 'feeling' approach. Thus, he carefully facilitates athlete autonomy (Cronin, Walsh, Quayle, Whittaker, & Whitehead, 2018). In addition, Terry uses technology to add value, prompt discussion and inform his care. This is a 'rules-based' conception of care, which has not been highly visible in Noddings' nurturing approach. Terry's story, therefore, extends the maternal notion of care by illustrating how rules-based science can add value and a different form of care to nurturing relationships. Data can prompt conversations that empower athletes; conversely, technology can be problematic and disempowering (Cronin et al., 2017). Thus, Terry's story has some interesting considerations for coaches, coach educators, coaching researchers and sport scientists to explore. Specifically:

1   There are times when coaches, with their knowledge, experience and 'coaching eye' are in the best place to care for an

athlete – e.g., avoiding overtraining. **Coaches**, therefore need to consider how and when they enact a 'duty of care' in their practice.

2   Authentic caring relationships are dialogical and consensual. Therefore, **coaches** should consider how they have gained consent for their care. Indeed, respecting the autonomy of athletes is not only ethical; it may also mitigate dependence, enabling athletes to 'self-care' and helping them to thrive in competition. Are athletes appropriately informed when consenting to coaching? Do coaches respect and facilitate the autonomous choices of athletes?

3   Developing caring relationships, which are dialogical and consensual, is a challenging and dynamic task. These relationships are contextual and influenced by both coaches and athletes. Thus as athletes develop, caring relationships should be 'scaffolded' over time. This requires **coaches** to consider what behaviours and language might coaches use in order to progressively foster caring relationships? How do they plan to develop caring relationships?

4   If used within reciprocal caring relationships, technology can be a useful means to an end (i.e. caring for athletes). Technology can, however, be used to control or dehumanise athletes. Thus, **coaches, coach educators** and **coach researchers** need to consider what technology is achieving within coaching practice, and how it can add value to caring relationships. Technology is likely to become more sophisticated, powerful and invasive over time. These questions, therefore, need to be asked repeatedly to ensure that technology adds value and does not distract from caring relationships.

5   **Sport scientists** often have technology, knowledge and skills that may enable them to care in a rule-based manner. How can sports scientists and coaches work together to develop caring strategies for athletes? What data is necessary to care for athletes? What do the athletes want and need? Can a rules-based approach to care be coupled with a pedagogical relationship? These are important and ongoing questions for **coaching researchers** and **sport science lecturers** to answer in order to help athletes flourish.

In sum, Terry's story illustrates that relationships are key to a caring pedagogy that helps athletes and coaches make better, more informed, decisions. His caring relationships have developed over time and are based on scaffolded dialogue, education and autonomy. Effective coaches, and indeed sport scientists, should therefore consider how they educate athletes to 'self-care.' For example, coaches and sport scientists could educate athletes about how to improve their diet, how to improve their sleep patterns or suggest ways they could warm their bodies up before training. Technology may be a prompt and aid for such caring pedagogy. After all, helping athletes to care for themselves might be the best use of the limited time that coaches and sport scientists have with athletes.

Note

1 An exception to this might be sport psychologists and lifestyle advisors who are often called in to help athletes with 'issues.'

Bibliography

Bunker, D., & Thorpe, R. (1982). A model for the teaching of games in the secondary school. *Bulletin of Physical Education, 18*(1), 9–16.

Cope, E., Partington, M., Cushion, C. J., & Harvey, S. (2016). An investigation of professional top-level youth football coaches' questioning practice. *Qualitative Research in Sport, Exercise and Health, 8*(4), 380–393. doi:10.1080/2159676X.2016.1157829

Côté, J., & Gilbert, W. (2009). An integrative definition of coaching effectiveness and expertise. *International Journal of Sports Science & Coaching, 4*(3), 307–323. doi:10.1260/174795409789623892

Côté, J., Young, B., North, J., & Duffy, P. (2007). Towards a definition of excellence in sport coaching. *International Journal of Coaching Science, 1*(1), 3–17.

Cronin, C., Walsh, B., Quayle, L., Whittaker, E., & Whitehead, A. (2018). Carefully supporting autonomy: Learning coaching lessons and advancing theory from women's netball in England. *Sports Coaching Review.* doi:10.1080/21640629.2018.1429113

Cronin, C., Whitehead, A. E., Webster, S., & Huntley, T. (2017). Transforming, storing and consuming athletic experiences: A coach's narrative of using a video application. *Sport, Education and Society*, 1–13. doi:10.1080/13573322.2017.1355784

Deci, E. L., & Ryan, R. M. (1985). *Intrinsic motivation and self-determination in human behaviour* (1st ed.). New York, NY: Plenum Press.

Denison, J., Mills, J. P., & Konoval, T. (2017). Sports' disciplinary legacy and the challenge of 'coaching differently'. *Sport, Education and Society, 22*(6), 772–783. doi:10.1080/13573322.2015.1061986

80   *Colum Cronin et al.*

Duda, J. L. (2013). The conceptual and empirical foundations of Empowering CoachingTM: Setting the stage for the PAPA project. *International Journal of Sport and Exercise Psychology, 11*(4), 311–318. doi:10.1080/1612197X.2013.839414

Fine, M., & Glendinning, C. (2005). Dependence, independence or interdependence? Revisiting the concepts of 'care' and 'dependency'. *Ageing and Society, 25*(4), 601–621. doi:10.1017/S0144686X05003600

Fraser-Thomas, J., & Côté, J. (2009). Understanding adolescents' positive and negative developmental experiences in sport. *The Sport Psychologist, 23*(1), 3–23. doi:10.1123/tsp.23.1.3

Gilligan, C. (1982). *In a different voice*. Boston, MA: Harvard.

Hargreaves, A., & Tucker, E. (1991). Teaching and guilt: Exploring the feelings of teaching. *Teaching and Teacher Education, 7*(5), 491–505. doi:10.1016/0742-051X(91)90044-P

Hedge, N., & MacKenzie, A. (2012). Beyond care? *Journal of Philosophy of Education, 46*(2), 192–207. doi:10.1111/j.1467-9752.2012.00844.x

Jones, C. M., Griffiths, P. C., & Melalieu, S. D. (2017). Training load and fatigue marker associations with injury and illness: A systematic review of longitudinal studies. *Sports medicine, 47*(5), 943–974. doi:10.1007/s40279-016-0619-5

Jones, R. L., & Thomas, G. L. (2015). Coaching as 'scaffolded' practice: Further insights into sport pedagogy. *Sports Coaching Review, 4*(2), 65–79. doi:10.1080/21640629.2016.1157321

Kennedy, P., & Kennedy, D. (2016). The role of sport science in the elite football labour process. *Sport, Business and Management: An International Journal, 6*(3), 341–359. doi:10.1108/SBM-07-2015-0023

Kidman, L., & Lombardo, B. (2010). *Athlete-centred coaching: Developing decision makers* (2nd ed.). Worcester, MA: IPC Print Resources.

Langdon, J., Harris, B. S., Burdette, III, G. P., & Rothberger, S. (2015). Development and implementation of an autonomy supportive training program among youth sport coaches. *International Sport Coaching Journal, 2*(2), 169–177. doi:10.1123/iscj.2014-0068

Mageau, G. A., & Vallerand, R. J. (2003). The coach: Athlete relationship: A motivational model. *Journal of Sport Sciences, 21*(11). doi:10.1080/0264041031000140374

Mosston, M. (1966). *Teaching physical education: From command to discovery*. London: MacMillan.

Nelson, L., Cushion, C. J., Potrac, P., & Groom, R. (2014). Carl Rogers, learning and educational practice: Critical considerations and applications in sports coaching. *Sport, Education and Society, 19*(5), 513–531. doi:10.1080/13573322.2012.689256

Noddings, N. (2005). *The challenge to care in schools: An alternative approach to education* (2nd ed.). New York, NY: Teachers College Press.

Noddings, N. (2013). *Caring; A relational approach to ethics and moral education* (2nd ed.). London: University of California Press.

Noddings, N. (2014). *Caring in education.* Retrieved from http://infed.org/mobi/caring-in-education/

Reid, M., Buszard, T., & Farrow, D. (2018). Learning, activity . . . and injury? Caring for young athletes through appropriately designed modified (developmental) sport. *British Journal of Sports Medicine.* doi:10.1136/bjsports-2017-098061

Taylor, W. G., & Garratt, D. (2010). The professionalisation of sports coaching: Relations of power, resistance and compliance. *Sport Education and Society, 15*(1), 121–139. doi:10.1080/13573320903461103

Tomkins, L., & Simpson, P. (2015). Caring leadership: A Heideggerian perspective. *Organization Studies*, 1–19. doi:0170840615580008

Williams, S., & Manley, A. (2016). Elite coaching and the technocratic engineer: Thanking the boys at Microsoft! *Sport, Education and Society, 21*(6), 828–850. doi:10.1080/13573322.2014.958816

6   Caring for, and with, others

Julie's story

Colum Cronin, Simon Roberts,
Owen Cronin and Kathleen Armour

Julie's story is prompted by a tension that coaches may experience between *caring about* sport performances and *caring for* athletes' health. In the UK, media reports and inquiries have suggested care for the athlete has been absent because of an overriding focus on winning (Grey-Thompson, 2017; UK Sport Independent Review Panel, 2017). I (Colum) have faced this ethical dilemma myself when asking players to 'dig deep' and go through the 'pain barrier' in order to win sporting tournaments. Interestingly, Julie's story raises this issue, but from a different perspective. Specifically, Julie's story describes incidents that she experienced as coach when her female athletes harmed themselves as a result of overtraining and under-eating in an attempt to improve their performances.

In keeping with previous chapters, an introduction to 'Julie' and her broad pedagogical context is followed by an initial analysis that explores these challenging issues by raising two further questions: 1) Are coaches equipped to care for athletes who are harming themselves? 2) How should coaches interact with other professionals in order to care for athletes effectively? To address these questions, in the analyses, Simon Roberts draws upon coach education literature to reflect upon what we know about the expertise and education of coaches. Dr Owen Cronin then offers a medical perspective on Julie's story by considering how coaches can work with other professionals to support athletes who may experience issues such as the 'female athlete triad.' Finally, the chapter concludes by highlighting key lessons learnt from Julie's story. These 'take-home' messages are provided for the benefit of coaches, coach developers and, ultimately, for athletes themselves.

Meet 'Julie'

Julie is an athletics coach in an endurance discipline. She has been a coach for over 15 years, and during our interviews, she struck me (Colum) as a 'real stalwart' of community sport. Her coaching experiences began with young children (10 years old upwards) in an after-school club in a rural village. At this club, Julie got to know the children and developed long-term training programmes that supported athletes as they progressed through their teenage years and through performance levels. She even coached her two children through the club. As Julie's athletes have developed, so has Julie's coaching career, including being involved in major international competitions such as the Commonwealth Games. She has fulfilled roles as a team manager helping with logistics and as a team coach working directly with athletes. She also fulfils a mentoring role with her national governing body that involves supporting coaches in their coaching environments. In more recent times, Julie has moved on from the local club. Now that her children have "grown up and moved out," she has moved from her rural location to a university town. This means she remains geographically close to her children. It has also enabled Julie to coach the running club at the university, which is a prestigious appointment.

Pedagogical context

Like the other coaches featured so far, Julie engages in pedagogical relationships with athletes. In her most recent role in a university, this pedagogical relationship involved undergraduate and postgraduate student-athletes who come to Julie in order to secure excellent running performances. Indeed, competitive excellence is the *raison d'etre* of Julie's relationships with students. For example, Julie declares:

> We have our varsity match this weekend, and it is over a hundred years old. It means more to the athletes than national championships or anything else. They are so focused on performing in this competition; it is their number one goal, and my job is to help them perform.

Within the context of competitive university sport, Julie does, however, retain a care ethic from her club coaching days:

I think our job as coaches is to make sure the athletes progress through to senior levels, and therefore I would say, you know, we have a duty of care to let them reach their potential, but not push them too hard.

I have had female middle-distance runners, and I have tried, to, um, kind of take care of whatever they needed, training wise, recovery wise. You know, if they needed ice bars, I'd take care of that.

Thus, Julie's story is about a coach who appreciates that caring relationships are an integral part of the coaching role. That does not mean, however, that caring is an easy act for Julie. On the contrary, the following narrative provides examples of times when Julie was challenged to care.

Julie's story

Midway through my (Colum) first interview with Julie, she began to ask me questions. For a few minutes, it felt as if she was interviewing me! Julie was eager to learn about my intentions for the research and showed some interest in my very modest attempts at running. Like many recreational runners, I had been doing some low mileage runs (3–5K) for health and relaxation purposes. My general pace and average distances were somewhat embarrassing compared to the high levels that Julie's athletes run. Nonetheless, she generously took the time to give me some advice about warming up and cooling down. With the best of intentions, Julie also suggested that as a beginning runner, my body might not be quite ready for a new activity. I took this comment in the supportive manner intended and noted her concerns about injury. Later in the interview, we also returned to the issue of injury prevention. Julie explained that she passes on similar advice to her runners at the start of each year in order to prevent physical injury and harm:

> Clearing acidosis from their legs is an important part of any session because it helps performance, recovery and athletes avoid injury. To help with this, the athletes (university level) have a gentle run that would be no more than 20 minutes. I have shown them stretches at the pre-season training camp or the first session,

and I expect them to do these stretches on their own after that run. With the younger athletes (early teens), I would ensure that together we stretched every muscle that we could think of at the end of the session. I do it with them to make sure they do it and know how to do it.

It surprised me that Julie would pass on such basic information to her high-performing runners. In subsequent interviews, once trust had built up between us, Julie explained why she was so concerned about injured athletes:

> It was sort of a general comment that did the damage. I (Julie) said to a young girl who had been progressing well, "Right you are a good athlete. You need to build up your mileage now." In response, this one particular athlete really took it upon herself to go for it and train really hard. She was at an age when her bones weren't properly formed. She was growing a lot, so her muscles were tight, and there were risks with increasing mileage in a maturing athlete. Had I known then what I know now, I wouldn't have allowed her to do that extra mileage. She got injured, and it really set her back. I worked it out as soon as she got injured, but it was too late then. She never developed as we hoped after that.

Although it occurred some time ago, it was clear to me that this incident has remained with Julie. In fact, Julie has invested significant time at courses and conferences in order to ensure she is informed enough to care for her athletes:

> A good coach always wants to better themselves and improve their knowledge, contacts and networking. You know, you learn just from chatting to other coaches and from conferences. We have sports science conferences, and we have conferences that cover the practical athletic side, as well. You are constantly learning, and the coach who does not keep in touch with up-to-date research will struggle at a higher level. To be frank, I think those who work with children as coaches need to know the kind of problems that things like maturation can bring. They need to know things like that so that they can do the best for their athletes. The position demands that coaches do their best for athletes.

Julie's actions are motivated by a desire to care for athletes. Additionally, Julie explained how she reviews training diaries on a weekly basis in order to ensure athletes are not overtraining. This concern for and interest in the athletes' needs is consistent with the concepts of engrossment and motivational displacement that Noddings' (2005) argues are the hallmarks of caring relationships. I asked Julie whether, she now feels better prepared to deal with the challenge of caring for maturing athletes. Julie was clear that while she is now more knowledgeable, she has come across new challenges while caring for university athletes. In particular, Julie is concerned with the eating habits of some of her athletes:

> I think sometimes you know if they're away from home and it's to do with, stressful academic environment. It's just a control thing. I don't know, but goodness me, it's hard as a coach to deal with. I personally had to ask this girl to stop coming, because I did not think it was correct for her to be doing any running. She had just lost so much weight. I only noticed it from a photograph on social media. Funnily enough, cos it's a bit like when you see people the whole time you don't necessarily see the small changes. But I just saw a photograph of her from one competition to the next. I remember thinking, "Oh she's lost quite a bit of weight." Unfortunately, it became very obvious after the academic holidays that she had a serious food problem. And it's hard dealing with something like that, because really, they need professional help.

Julie's revelations took me by surprise. I had not come across these specific issues in my sport or my athletes. Nonetheless, Julie assured me that it was increasingly a common issue in running. Julie introduced me to the term 'female athlete triad,' which refers to a tripartite of medical conditions: amenorrhea, disordered eating and osteoporosis. The fact that my coaching experiences were almost entirely with male populations explains why I had not come across this term. From this position of ignorance, however, I asked Julie to explain more about the phenomenon. She provided me with a dramatic story of supporting athletes who suffer from this condition:

> Sometimes, it could be a nutritional issue, but quite often, it can be a psychological problem. It seemed to be psychological in

this case. An underlying psychological issue can manifest itself in poor nutrition, and I was aware of this. I think it's crucial to get the right people, and normally I might give an athlete encouragement and say, "I'll let you come to training" or "I'll let you do this competition, if you show me that you put on a couple of pounds." But this girl was at such a severe risk of fracture that I had to ask her to stop training and go see a doctor. Actually, it was the captain of the club who said, "We should stop her." It has to be a team effort with the captain, the doctor and her parents. I provided them with as much information as I could about the dangers of what was happening to her. The first port of call is see your doctor. Hopefully, if you're in an area that has, you know, good therapy nearby, erm, they can be put in touch with those people, whether it's the nutritionist or a psychologist because (yeah) quite often it can be, erm, sort of slight psychological problem.

This story illustrates a growing problem for coaches and, as the next section demonstrates, offers both positive and negative learning opportunities.

Initial analysis by Colum Cronin

Julie's story is an example of a coach who has developed her caring practice over time. She has sought more knowledge continuously throughout her career. These learning behaviours were prompted by reflections on a critical incident where an athlete suffered negative effects from overtraining. This route to coach learning has been reported extensively in the literature (e.g. Gilbert & Trudel, 2002; Knowles, Borrie, & Telfer, 2005; Nash & Sproule, 2011; Cropley, Miles, & Peel, 2012). Case studies also have shown that reflective practice can help coaches to connect theory with pedagogical practice (Cropley et al., 2012) and how coaches learn from reflecting upon experiences throughout their career (Irwin, Hanton, & Kerwin, 2004; Rynne & Mallet, 2012; Mead, Spencer, & Kidman, 2016). Consistent with these cases, Julie has learnt how to care for athletes from her prior experience of coaching in a rural athletics club.

Notwithstanding Julie's experiences, it is important to recognise that learning from negative incidents can also be an ineffective and even unethical approach to the development of caring coaching practices. The aim must be to prevent the negative incidents that prompted Julie's reflection in the first place – i.e., before the damage is done to young athletes. Additionally, although often described as an internal cognitive process, reflective practice is not 'neutral' in that it is situated and historically informed act. Cushion (2016) has argued that the social contexts that frame coaches' practice and reflection upon that practice could lead to the uncritical reproduction of taken-for granted-behaviours, stifling innovation and the creation of new knowledge. Thus, in climates where uncaring practice is perpetuated and normalised, or where care is not explicitly valued, reflective practice may not be the best mechanism for learning.

It was reassuring to note that Julie has also engaged in a wide variety of learning opportunities beyond formal coaching courses to ensure that she can care for athletes who may suffer physically or psychologically. Conferences and seminars on topics such as the female athlete triad have been particularly useful for Julie, some of which crosses specific sport activities. In effect, Julie has moved beyond her day-to-day coaching context to learn how best to care for athletes. This is interesting because Purdy, Potrac and Paulauskas (2016, p. 221) suggest that coaches may need knowledge "beyond the 'nuts and bolts' of sporting performance" and may need knowledge of existential and social issues. This prompted me to consider whether formal coach education programmes equip coaches fully to care for athletes. In the disciplinary perspectives section that follows, Simon Roberts will consider this question by drawing on coach education literature.

On a similar theme, Julie's story also prompted me to consider whether coaches are best placed to care for athletes. Julie's story suggests there are limits to her expertise in this area, and this could have negative consequence for athletes in need of care. Even when Julie has developed further as a coach, there was a point at which she felt it was appropriate to engage with other individuals in order to care for an athlete. Fortunately, for the athlete concerned, Julie's informal learning helped her to recognise the limits of her competence in this area. In response, Julie called upon her team captain, the athlete's parents and medical professionals to provide additional care for the athlete. In so doing, she ensured the athlete was surrounded by a multidisciplinary climate of care,[1] wherein a community of individuals exhibit caring disposition (Gano-Overway, 2014).

Gano-Overway argues that by modelling caring dispositions such as engrossment, empathy and motivational displacement, coaches can prompt and encourage others to also care for athletes. This approach appears to be an example of best practice in that it recognises the limitations of individual coaches to care, while still ensuring that athletes receive appropriate care. That said, Gano-Overway also suggests that to develop a caring team and a caring climate, coaches must explicitly and intentionally demonstrate care, draw attention to their caring acts and facilitate care. In a coaching context, this could include demonstrating care to athletes, parents, fellow staff, and governing bodies. Given the noted absence of care in some high-profile coaching contexts, caring climates may not be as prevalent as they should be. Indeed, it appears that many coaches may not currently be provided with sufficient information on how to work with others in a caring climate.

Therefore, the first analysis Simon Roberts considers care within formal coach education. As an experienced coach, coach educator and academic, Simon utilises both his own experiences and extant literature to consider how formal coach education prepares coaches to care. In the second disciplinary perspective that follows, Dr Owen Cronin similarly reflects upon Julie's story. Owen draws upon his medical experience of working with coaches to care for athletes who may suffer from issues such as those related to the female athlete triad.

Theoretical perspective 1: coach learning – how can coaches develop as professionals who care for others?
Simon Roberts

When reading Julie's story, my (Simon) initial thoughts transmitted me back to my early experiences of learning how to teach PE. As a novice teacher, I recall efforts back then to transform the teacher education context with a movement away from traditional formal supervisory models, to what we now understand as informal, in situ 'professional development' programmes. It was during these collaborations with colleagues from nearby secondary schools, local authorities, health agencies and other associated organisations (i.e. children's social services) that I was first exposed to professional role-related competencies that extended beyond my declarative and procedural PE knowledge.

Back in 1994–1995, my training had followed a traditional competency based model where I was effectively told what to do and how to do it. The professional development programme however introduced other aspects of the pupil–teacher relationship that, hitherto, I had not encountered (or considered) during my apprenticeship in university-based teacher training. For example, it was the first time I was urged to give serious consideration to the possibility of a child suffering from associated forms of abuse or neglect. As a young teacher of PE, I was encouraged to be alert (especially when the pupils were changing into their PE uniforms) for signs of unusual bruising, scratches, cuts and swellings. When I suspected unusual injuries or a dramatic change in pupil behaviour, I was trained in the art of asking non-leading questions as the requirement of my duties extended to that of a *carer*. My role required me to act 'in loco parentis' – in other words – I had a duty of care. For Armour and Jones (1998), such actions represent the transition and distinction between caring *about* pupils to caring *for* pupils. Interestingly, when considering Julie's case, eating disorders were not included as a condition we needed to be aware of at the time. Similar to Colum's initial analysis earlier, this may have been due to the assumption that only females suffer with eating disorders.

As illustrated in Julie's story, issues around neglect can lead to unfortunate moments for the athlete. Unfortunately, we as coaches, teachers and volunteers are not always aware of *how best to care*. To elucidate the point, I once more take you back to my early days as a teacher of PE. I recall it as follows:

> In the school where I once worked, I recall we utilised the services of one of the music teachers, Jim (a pseudonym). Jim used to help out on a volunteer basis running various extra-curricular clubs and had responsibility for coaching and managing one of the boys' football and cricket teams. There was one occasion, however, due to unfortunate staff illness, where my head of department asked Jim whether he was willing to be the member of staff at a pre-organised inter-school netball match. To avoid cancelling the fixture, the visiting school offered to supply both officials all they asked in return for a member of the teaching staff to be present at the side of the court. Jim kindly agreed.
>
> A keenly fought game was drawing to a close when one of our girls contested a high-ball and inadvertently got flipped over her

opponents back, landing heavily on the concrete playing surface. Sensing the seriousness of the situation, Jim raced onto the court and knelt down beside the injured player who was screaming in pain, blood flowing down her thigh. She was in obvious distress, and in order to make her more comfortable and to stem the flow of blood, Jim grabbed a loose netball bib and placed it, within his hand, on the top of the players' thigh. Eventually, an ambulance was called, and the player was taken to hospital. Jim was visibly shaken by events, but he was reassured by the offers of support he had received from a small smattering of parents who were watching the game and said he had helped. The following day, however, Jim was summoned to the headmaster's office because the parents of the injured player had issued a formal complaint. Following this incident, the local authority instigated new guidelines to all teachers of physical education that in the case of pupil injury – staff must request permission and consent to touch the pupil before administering any first aid. In the case of Jim, he was reprimanded for not asking the injured player whether he could lift up her netball skirt to stem the flow of blood.

As an epilogue to this tale, Jim didn't volunteer his services to help out the department again. Some would argue that Jim acted in a caring, considerate manner, acting on instinct in order to minimise the pain and seriousness of the injury. Twenty-three years on from this incident taking place, I wonder how many sport coaches today would know how to care in such a scenario? Would or should they respond differently to Jim?

In contrast to Jim's experiences, Julie's story highlights the lack of care afforded in high-profile coaching contexts. Despite the emergence of dual pathways and awards for specific age group and contexts offered by some national governing bodies (i.e. coaching children awards and coaching young people and adults awards), I would argue the same can be said for participation contexts in community based settings. For example, there is a shortage of research surrounding how sport coaches and sports clubs facilitate the notion of 'care' in their acceptance of disadvantaged or socially vulnerable children (Haudenhuyse, Theeboom, & Nols, 2013). Despite knowing that participation in sport provides a powerful tool for engaging young people in organised contexts, with evidence positively suggesting departures from antisocial behaviour and criminal activities, we have limited information about the effective development of these relationships and the role played by the sport coach. An exception to this is the work conducted by Haudenhuyse, Theeboom, Nols and Coussée (2014) whereby young Flemish people who were considered socially vulnerable were interviewed about their motivations for participating in sport. In the context of this chapter, this study is interesting for a number of reasons. First, socially vulnerable youths who suffer with negative self-image, a lack of future prospects, negative experiences of educational institutions and a fragile social network revealed that it was the caring nature of the sport coach, which played a central role in creating a powerful and positive outlook. What struck me though was how the young people who were interviewed talked about wanting a coach who "they could talk to" and "a coach who took the time to understand and step into young people's world outside the sports club" (Haudenhuyse et al., 2014, p. 187) as crucial reasons for maintaining an interest in sport. Second, the take-home messages for staying within a sport-based setting were based on social reasons, the caring nature of the relationships with their coaches and the enjoyment of playing sports. This may sound like common sense, but often in competitive mainstream sports where result-orientated outcomes are implicitly engrained as part of the club culture, it could lead to the promotion of aggression and violence. For some groups (especially the socially or medically vulnerable), this could be the type of culture they are trying to escape and may act as a barrier to engaging in sport and physical activity. Again, I wonder how well prepared coaches are to care for such athletes.

Can formal coach education help coaches to care?

As someone who used to work as a coach education tutor for a large national governing body of sport, and as someone who currently works in academia, I (Simon) am fully aware of the criticism(s) which have been levelled at formal coach education provision (Nelson, Cushion, & Potrac, 2013). Some of this criticism, such as the evidence base for enhanced coach learning, is seemingly justified (i.e. Chesterfield, Potrac, & Jones, 2010). However, I also think we need to be realistic about what can be achieved in the delivery of formal education, especially when one considers the constraints imposed by frameworks, national qualification standards and funding. Nevertheless, issues such as how coaching process competencies encountered during formal education are assessed continues to be problematic and needs to be addressed (Lyle & Cushion, 2016). I can say with some authority that during my time as a coach educator, the issues raised in Julie's story were not covered in any of the course material or in the mandatory child protection and safeguarding components of the award. The notion of the 'caring coach' is perhaps a good example of a 'softer skill,' which currently lies outside role-related competencies traditionally assessed as part of a coach education certificate. This state of affairs is not easily explained, especially when one considers how athlete–player support and development lies at the heart of the coach–athlete relationship and coaching practice.

In order to address some of these issues, I agree with Lyle and Cushion (2016) in that I would like to see coach education consider more innovative modes of developing a coach's operational behaviour. I have written about this previously (Roberts & Ryrie, 2014), and I am left wondering whether Julie had covered a pedagogical case scenario (Armour, 2017), where overtraining, eating disorders and the female triad were presented. For me, this context, in situ based assessment, offers an alternative and more realistic solution to some of the sport-based competencies (i.e. techniques and tactics) or portfolios of progressive session plans currently en vogue with national governing bodies of sport. I suspect that as Lyle and Cushion (2016) suggest, logistics of time and tutor workforce expertise could make this aspiration problematic, but at the very least, there should be a more authentic and contextualised opportunity for a coach to articulate how he or she deals with particular caring challenges through his or her situated experience.

With the notion of authentic care-focused coach education in mind, I am reminded of my experiences as a parent. Most weekends, I watch my son (11 years of age) participate in a grassroots football (soccer) environment. He has a qualified coach who volunteers, giving freely of his time during the week (i.e. training) and at the weekend (competition). This does not take into account the number of unseen organisational hours liaising with other teams, parents, results secretaries, referees, etc. He mentioned to me recently how the assessment for his next coach award included a portfolio of coaching sessions, and yet most weeks, he has to deal with problems normally associated with unacceptable abusive behaviour towards an official or players either from a parent or from another member of the coaching team. From the perspective of the 'caring' coach, finding a resolution to these issues is far more pertinent in terms of a supportive environment than whether the team plays a *tiki-taka* style of football or executes a high forward press. However, until this element of coaching practice (i.e. care) is afforded the necessary time and attention, I suspect he will not have access to authentic formal 'care education.' Regretfully, care remains a concept that is on the periphery of formal coach education and coach training. Coach educators should therefore, consider how to address this situation.

Theoretical perspective 2; a medical perspective: how can coaches and medical professionals care for athletes together? Dr Owen Cronin

As I (Owen) read Julie's study, it reminded me of the central purpose of sports and exercise medicine. Specifically, the medical speciality is tasked with the responsibility of caring for athletes of all levels and the promotion of physical activity for health improvement in the general population. In practice, this means that many consultants in sports medicine, or doctors with a special interest in sports medicine, will encounter cases similar to Julie's story. Awareness of the female athlete triad has therefore increased amongst medical professionals, and Julie's story suggests knowledge of this condition has begun to permeate to the grassroots and university coaching levels.

For readers not familiar with the condition, the term 'female athlete triad' has recently been amended to reflect the occurrence of this phenomenon in males. The term Relative Energy Deficiency in Sport (RED-S) is now accepted by medical professionals, and the condition is characterised by a low body weight, fatigue, lack of motivation and underperformance, often in the presence of reduced bone mineral density (osteoporosis), irregular or absent menstruation (females) and disordered eating habits (e.g. anorexia nervosa) (Statuata, Asif, & Drezner, 2017). RED-S is particularly prevalent in aesthetic sports (e.g. gymnastics) but also occurs prominently in endurance sports where body composition has a significant impact on performance outcomes (Claessens, Lefevre, Beunen, & Malina, 1999). Thus, it is not surprising, though unfortunate, that Julie encountered an athlete suffering with this condition. Indeed, Julie's story is a valuable example that may help other coaches recognise the RED-S condition.

Julie's story not only provides an example of the RED-S condition but also illustrates a clear example of the ever-increasing role that sports science and sports medicine play in the success and lives of elite and aspiring athletes. Specifically, later in the narrative, when Julie is more experienced, she recognises the limits of her caring abilities. She successfully broached the need for medical input with the athlete and her family. This suggests to me that her athletes respect her opinion. Gold standard care of athletes suffering from RED-S is multidisciplinary in nature, often requiring input from nutritionists, endocrinologists, psychologists and sports medicine physicians – a web of care akin to a caring climate (see Chapter 2 for further discussion on caring climates) (Gano-Overway, 2014). In addition, the athlete's coach can be an integral component of successful treatment outcomes provided an agreed treatment plan be arranged by athlete, coach and physician. Once a plan is in place, focus and energy should be assigned to implementing this plan. To do so, clear communication is required. I believe it is often a useful practice for coaches to attend doctors' appointments with their athletes (provided patient consent is provided). This allows for regular review and ensures that all parties are in unison. In my experience, although it may be a biased perception, the player or coach most often breaks this treatment plan. In the coach's case, this is usually due to a combination of external pressures and their own internal ambitions (O'Neill, 2016). Nonetheless, it is reassuring from reading Julie's story that some coaches are aware of sporting-related medical issues that can affect athletes' lives and health beyond their sport.

In contrast to Julie's story, and despite a shared common goal of competitive success, coach–doctor relationships can be antagonistic. This is because treatment for RED-S or the female athlete triad and other conditions can require a reduction and modification of training and competition workload, which can often lead to conflict and disagreement between the athlete, coach and medical team. Personally, I have provided medical care for teams where direct pressure is placed on athletes to return to sport despite their injuries and illnesses. In addition, I have also experienced situations where indirect and covert pressure is placed on medical teams to declare an athlete fit for competition. My personal opinion is that a successful coach–doctor

relationship is founded on respect initially, followed by clear identification and agreement of each party's individual roles and goals
and, finally, their execution through appropriate behaviours. My own
approach was to try to meet with the head coach before commencing
a post, outlining these issues while acknowledging a commitment to
have athletes available for training and competition as much as possible. One strategy I employ is to try to convince the coach that it is
in the team's interests (and likewise in the coach's and athlete's interests) that injury or illness may lead to irreparable damage or shorten-
ing of an athlete's career with the team, ultimately to the detriment
of the organisation. This is particularly apt in the case of the RED-S,
where Julie's athlete will require ongoing technical and psychological support for many years to come, of which the coach is probably
best placed to provide some aspects of care.

Notwithstanding the vital influence that coaches may have in caring for athletes, it is important that coaches recognise both their
own limitations and occasions when medical or psychological care
needs to be escalated to the appropriate health-care professionals
(e.g. ongoing disordered eating, new stress fracture). For example,
it can be difficult for a coach to approach an athlete with a health
concern and it requires tactfulness, sensitivity and, perhaps, medical expertise. The appropriateness of such interactions may also be
questionable – e.g., a male coach asking a female athlete about her
reproductive health. Similarly, removing athletes from the field of
play, or indeed declaring them unfit for play, is an extremely challenging aspect of any coach role. It can be difficult for athletes to
accept their illnesses, particularly when they are a direct result of
excessive training. Athletes will employ strategies to avoid this real-
ity. Care and tact, coupled with some medical knowledge, are therefore required, and while I do not know for certain, I would imagine
coaches do not receive much training on how best to approach these
medical issues.

In my opinion, coach education is key to improving athlete health.
Coaches can be professional, highly skilled mentors for athletes who
interact with them on a frequent basis. Coaches are in a unique position to recognise health concerns in athletes and to prevent progression to irreparable harm. They should be facilitated in this regard.
That said, athletes and their coaches are often confined to a focus
'bubble' of complete commitment to training, recovery and competition. Within this 'bubble,' gradual physical and psychological changes

in athletes may be missed, and negative health effects may go unnoticed. One strategy that could be employed to avoid this would be the use of structured and formal reflection (reflection sessions) whereby the health of their athletes is discussed and considered periodically by the coaching team. In doing so, care would become an overt part of every session evaluation.

Implications from Julie's story

Julie's story illustrates a holistic approach to care, where coaches consider the wider health of athletes. As Owen alludes to in his analysis from a sport medicine perspective, coaches spend significant time periods with athletes and are in a position to recognise the signs, symptoms and wider physical, psychological and social challenges that athletes face. Coaches are also well placed to support athletes through recovery by helping athletes adhere to treatment plans. Conversely, as Simon describes, extant formal coach education tends to be decontextualised and deal with care through a minimum standards approach. Difficult care scenarios that do not relate to sport techniques and tactics are rarely covered, particularly at lower levels of qualification. This means that coaches may not be well prepared to address the complex, relational and unique care needs of athletes. Thus, Julie's story illustrates the paradox that coaches are both well placed but also under-educated to care for athletes. This conclusion raises some interesting questions for coaches, coach educators and coaching researchers to explore. Specifically:

- Practicing coaches and coaching students need to consider their own care skills. As part of performance reviews or self-reflective practices, coaches should consider their knowledge. Can they recognise the negative effects of sport participation and performance? Do they have the skills to deal with unforeseen care challenges? Where could they access more learning opportunities that would help them to care more effectively and holistically?
- Coach educators may need to reconsider how they support coaches develop as carers. For example, do coaches have resources to draw upon that can prompt discussions, and inform good caring practices? Do coach assessments consider how coaches develop caring coach–athlete relationships, or are coach assessments focused on the transmission of technical and tactical skills?

- As Simon describes in his analysis, coach education has been much criticised for decontextualised activities and simplified assessments. In response, some organisations have begun to include in situ assessments of coaching and problem based learning. This provides coach educators with opportunities to observe how coaches work with others (parents, athletes, fellow staff, stakeholders) to create a web of care in their own training and competition environments. Do coach assessments include analysis of how coaches encourage parents, fellow coaches and medical staff to create caring environments? This question is pertinent, because creating a caring environment should be a precursor to athletes flourishing.
- Coach researchers also have an opportunity to improve care in sport. For example, coach educators need evidence on how to develop caring relationships, caring climates and how to deal with complex issues that might require care. To that end, coach researchers should seek to inform formal coach education by considering what can be learnt about care from other professions – e.g., teaching, social work, medicine.
- Julie's story also illustrates that good caring practice can be developed through trial and error, and non-formal learning. Coach researchers should seek to capture the wisdom of experienced coaches such as Julie and use it to inform practice. This book is a significant step in this direction, but it could be built upon with the development of workshops, training programmes, models of caring coaching and sport policy informed by caring approach to coaching. In sum, Julie's story raises the question of how best can coaches be educated about care and supported to enact care.

Note

1 Discussed previously in Chapter 2.

Bibliography

Armour, K. M. (2017). Pedagogical cases: A new translational mechanism to bridge theory/research practice gaps in youth physical activity education (PAE). *Kinesiology Review*, 6(1), 42–50. doi:10.1123/kr.2016-0037

Armour, K. M., & Jones, R. (1998). *Physical education teachers' lives and careers* (1st ed.). London: Falmer Press.

Chesterfield, G., Potrac, P., & Jones, R. (2010). 'Studentship' and 'impression management' in an advanced soccer coach education award. *Sport, Education and Society*, *15*(3), 299–314. doi:10.1080/13573322.2010.49 3311

Claessens, A. L., Lefevre, J., Beunen, G., & Malina, R. M. (1999). The contribution of anthropometric characteristics to performance scores in elite female gymnasts. *Journal of Sports Medicine and Physical Fitness*, *39*(4), 355–360.

Cropley, B., Miles, A., & Peel, J. (2012). *Reflective practice: Value of, issues, and developments with sports coaching.* Leeds: Sports Coach UK.

Cushion, C. J. (2016). Reflection and reflective practice discourses in coaching: A critical analysis. *Sport, Education and Society*. doi:10.1080/ 13573322.2016.1142961

Gano-Overway, L. A. (2014). The caring climate: How sport environments can develop empathy in young people. In K. Pavlovich, & K. Krahnke (Eds.), *Organising through empathy* (pp. 166–183). New York, NY: Routledge.

Gilbert, W. D., & Trudel, P. (2002). Learning to coach through experience: Reflection in model youth sport coaches. *Journal of Teaching in Physical Education*, *21*(1), 16–34. doi:10.1123/jtpe.21.1.16

Grey-Thompson, T. (2017). *Duty of care in sport.* London: Independent Report to Government.

Haudenhuyse, R., Theeboom, M., & Nols, Z. (2013). Sports-based interventions for socially vulnerable youth: Towards well-defined interventions with easy-to-follow outcomes? *International Review for the Sociology of Sport*, *48*(4), 471–484. doi:10.1177/1012690212448002

Haudenhuyse, R., Theeboom, M., Nols, Z., & Coussée, F. (2014). Socially vulnerable young people in Flemish sports clubs: Investigating youth experiences. *European Physical Education Review*, *20*(2), 179–198. doi:10.1177/1356336X13508686

Irwin, G., Hanton, S., & Kerwin, D. (2004). Reflective practice and the origins of elite coaching knowledge. *Reflective Practice: International and Multidisciplinary Perspectives*, *5*(3), 425–442. doi:10.1080/14623 94042000270718

Knowles, Z., Borrie, A., & Telfer, H. (2005). Towards the reflective sports coach: Issues of context, education and application. *Ergonomics*, *48*(11), 1711–1720. doi:10.1080/00140130500101288

Lyle, J., & Cushion, C. (2016). *Sports coaching concepts: A framework for coaching practice.* London: Routledge.

Mead, S., Spencer, K., & Kidman, L. (2016). Video self-reflection and coach development in New Zealand. *Asia-Pacific Journal of Health, Sport and Physical Education, 7*(2), 139–156. doi:10.1080/18377122.2016.1196113

Nash, C. S., & Sproule, J. (2011). Insights into Experiences: Reflections of an expert and novice coach. *International Journal of Sports Science & Coaching, 6*(1), 149–162. doi:10.1260/1747-9541.6.1.149

Nelson, L., Cushion, C., & Potrac, P. (2013). Enhancing the provision of coach education: The recommendations of UK coaching practitioners. *Physical Education and Sport Pedagogy, 18*(2), 204–218. doi:10.1080/17408989.2011.649725

Noddings, N. (2005). *The challenge to care in schools: An alternative approach to education* (2nd ed.). New York, NY: Teachers College Press.

O'Neill, L. (2016). "No way Jose!" Clinicians must have authority over patient care: The manager's scope of practice does not cover medical decisions. *British Journal of Sports Medicine, 50*(5), 259. doi:10.1136/bjsports-2015-095420

Purdy, L., Potrac, P., & Paulauskas, R. T. (2016). Nel Noddings. In L. Nelson, R. Groom, & P. Potrac (Eds.), *Learning in sports coaching: Theory and application* (pp. 215–227). Oxon: Routledge.

Roberts, S., & Ryrie, A. (2014). Socratic case-method teaching in sports coach education: Reflections of students and course tutors. *Sport, Education and Society, 19*(1), 63–79. doi:10.1080/13573322.2011.632626

Rynne, S. B., & Mallet, C. J. (2012). Understanding the work and learning of high performance coaches. *Physical Education and Society*, 507–523. doi:10.1080/17408989.2011.621119

Statuata, S. M., Asif, I. M., & Drezner, J. A. (2017). Relative energy deficiency in sport (RED-S). *British Journal of Sports Medicine, 51*(21), 1570–1571. doi:10.1136/bjsports-2017-097700

UK Sport Independent Review Panel. (2017). *Report into the climate and culture of the world class programme in British Cycling.* London: UK Sport.

7 The cost of caring

Dave's story

Colum Cronin, John Hayton,
Sören Hjälm and Kathleen Armour

At our first interview, I (Colum) immediately connected with Dave. Like me, Dave is a basketball coach. That said, in addition to his role as a coach in a school, he has coached at a much higher level than I do: county teams, national championships and international teams. He has even had successful teams at major international championships, which is far beyond my own modest coaching achievements. Despite his lofty success, during our interviews, Dave is generous with his time and helpful. I am not surprised, therefore, when Dave explains how he often spends time supporting teenage basketball players and their families:

> Players' mums sometimes ring me (Dave) up and say, "Look he (the athlete) has been foolish at home. Can you have a word?" So, I have word and say, "Get your act together. Do I have to take basketball away from you to get the point across?" Normally, it works straight away, and from that point of view, the parents are finding it very helpful.

Dave's emphasis on positive youth development reflects his day job as a basketball coach in a school. Within this role, he teaches basketball to all the children (ages 13–16) at an inner-city high school. He predominantly teaches them basic skills, but he does so in order to achieve outcomes associated with the national curriculum such as improving performance and educating young people to lead healthy lives (Department for Education, 2013). In addition to these aims, Dave is very keen to develop 'good character' through basketball. He provides examples of meeting parents after coaching sessions to discuss the behaviour of players and meetings with families in their homes to support young people when they are choosing university. Through these stories, Dave emphasises the potential to use basketball as a vehicle that has a positive influence on young people's wider social development:

> Some of our kids are very difficult to handle in a classroom. A lot of the kids have done well just to stay in school. There have been quite a few success stories given the background they are coming from. Single parent families, socioeconomic problems, living in tough areas that are not safe. That kind of thing. But on a basketball court, they are really committed. And, basically, cause of the power of the game and their love of the game, these kids will basically do anything I want them to do, or ask them to do. From that point of view, I get a lot of respect from the teaching staff and particularly senior management.

Thus, Dave straddles two distinct basketball contexts (Côté, Young, North, & Duffy, 2007). In the evenings and weekends, he works with very talented young athletes who are part of a national talent development pathway. For this work, Dave receives modest remuneration.[1] So during weekdays, Dave works with children who have a more recreational approach to basketball in a setting with a mass participation focus. His work in schools provides Dave with a sustainable income akin to a PE teacher. This does, however, mean that Dave leads a very busy coaching life. Caring for the holistic development of players in both school and high-performance contexts is an intensive and time-consuming labour, which has some negative influences upon Dave's personal and social life:

> You know my schedule is crazy. This is something that is the one thing that annoys her (his partner). If I come back from training and I am late by half an hour, it could be because I am talking to a parent about a player's performance at school. My partner finds that frustrating. She is always saying, "You know you have your family too. They need to take care of their own kids."

On this theme, the narrative which follows explores how caring for athletes and caring about sport performance can have negative implications for coaches and their families. To explore these issues further, the narrative is followed by two disciplinary analyses. Firstly, John Hayton draws on sociological literature to consider caring in sport coaching as an emotional labour. Secondly, Sören Hjälm considers Dave's story from a psychological perspective and draws upon wider literature that explores burnout in coaches. As with the other stories in the previous three chapters (Jane, Terry and Julie), this chapter concludes by summarising key take-home messages. These messages are valuable for coach educators, employers and coaches themselves, because if coaching is to be recognised as a legitimate caring activity, then caring must become a sustainable ethic for coaches.

Dave's story

After much time discussing basketball and sharing our views, Dave began to talk to me (Colum) in a more personal manner. This occurred during our third interview. Prior to this point, Dave was relentlessly positive and professional. He had described exhilarating experiences while coaching national teams, outlined the generous support provided by the school where he teachers and detailed how much he enjoys building relationships with athletes. It was, therefore, a surprising shift in tone when Dave confessed:

> I will be honest with you. Sometimes, it takes up so much of my time. 'Cause I kind of feel I have to follow through with a lot of social support. You know 'cause otherwise I feel what we are doing with the basketball academy is ineffective. If I am not making sure they are 'toeing the line' in lessons or around the school, then I am not being totally effective. But that is time consuming.

I sensed Dave wanted to open up about the demands of his role, and he went on to declare:

> I am getting inundated with emails every day. If there is a problem with a kid in a history lesson, they won't email the form tutor, they will email me. If he has a basketball academy tie on, I will get an email saying so and so hasn't done his homework or so and so is playing up in my lesson. Really what they should be doing is emailing the form tutor, but it has become the situation

now. That is not formally done, but it has come about this way. They contact me now instead of the form tutor.

It is clear that the pastoral care of young people is a significant part of Dave's coaching role and one that is demanding. Dave's concerns about the extent of this pastoral care and its effects on his wider personal life resonated with my own experiences as a lecturer who also coached youth basketball in the evenings after work and at weekends. I was regularly unable to spend weekends with family. I have missed birthdays, anniversaries and other important occasions. For me, basketball coaching has often led to a tension between my duty to care for players and to be with family and friends. Dave also experienced this tension:

> I (Dave) was married to a woman who hated sport, and basketball is in my heart. I'd never leave the sport you know, and she didn't want to share me with basketball. We went our separate ways because I was involved with the national team. In fact, at the time I was just getting involved, and it was a constant battle every day. Even going out to practice on a Saturday morning was a challenge, and she couldn't understand, she didn't understand our culture. She didn't understand that our way of life is to be out at every weekend. She had never been exposed to it.
>
> (Cronin & Armour, 2017, p. 928)

Although, I could empathise with Dave, I have not shared his experience of international basketball. In order to understand the tension between the demands of coaching at that level and sustaining familial relationships, I asked Dave to explain what a typical national team-coaching weekend is like:

> We had Sweden here for a tournament last weekend. It was a pre-European preparation series, series of games really, erm. We played them on Friday night; we played them on Saturday night, and we played them on Sunday, erm, early evening. But on top of the games, we had 2-hour practice Friday, 2-hour practice Saturday and then 90-minute practice on Sunday. And on top of the practices, we had two, no four, no we had five video analysis sessions and in between those times, we had player individual meetings. And on the Friday, we had positional meetings and again

on the Saturday. We had another team meeting on the Sunday. It was very taxing for me, because I was looking over my shoulder every two seconds, basically I was under surveillance from the GB performance director.

When recounting these experiences, Dave explicitly acknowledged the demanding nature of the coaching lifestyle. It was clear that he cared deeply about the team, success and sport. I was surprised by the amount of time that Dave spends with players off the basketball court. Indeed, a large section of his weekend was spent in meetings and in video sessions with players where he "got to know them" so that he was able to care for and about their sporting development. These days, I have reduced my own coaching workload, and I do not invest as much time as Dave in developing relationships with athletes in this manner. I am acutely aware that weekends such as this would be at the expense of my own familial relationships, and it is a price that I have not been prepared to pay. In contrast, Dave was in a reflective mood and rather than regret spending so much time coaching, he began to lament not starting his coaching career even earlier:

> You know one assistant coach at the national team is only 22 and is pretty top for his age. I said to him, "Look, you're not attached. Why don't you pursue a job overseas? Just for a year." And you know, so he's going over to the States soon. I wish, I always wish, I'd have done it sooner, like him. But I was still chasing the days of playing. I thought that I was a better player at 25, but I was no longer as good as I was when I was 20. And as I got towards 30, I still thought, "The body is going to feel better." But the body never heals like it used to, so you know you chase your playing days up until your late 20s. Then the body's gone, and the back is gone, and you start coaching.

It was clear from this answer that Dave was engrossed in basketball to a level that I was not. He had clearly decided to invest his time in his coaching; he cared about basketball, and he cared deeply for his athletes. Yet, he also recognised the cost of caring about his sport and caring for athletes upon his wider social relationships:

> I was away all Summer. I came back on the 31 of August, we returned to school on the 1st of September. We had no holidays. That

takes a lot of support from families. A lot of understanding. So from that point of view, I'm very lucky with my new partner. I was listening to my staff, while we were away at a camp. I just came home and thanked her: "Thank you for being so understanding, because when I heard these guys, what they were going through with their wives . . ." Not all of them, some of them, it's – I remember how it used to be from years ago, you know, with a different partner.

Dave's story is underpinned by his choice to care about sport and care for players and the consequences of this choice for his wider relationships. Other coaches involved in this book also told similar stories. For example, Julie (see Chapter 6) declared:

> You know my relationship broke down (yeah) because I was away so much coaching. No, there are all sorts of reasons, but you know, coaching didn't help. I don't know whether it's because I'm female or what, but I've decided that now I have to have a balance between my coaching and my home life (yeah). I think if you're going to be a professional coach, it is almost a 24-hour day job. I'm sure there are people who manage with a partner to do that, but I don't think I'd be very good at it.

Jane (see Chapter 4) also reflected on the cost of coaching for her family life:

> My parents love hearing about coaching when I get back, but they don't necessarily want me going off all the time as much as I do. I think they see that I don't get the opportunities to go on holiday because this is the time of year I am coaching. And we do have a little place over in North Wales that I would love to go to more often. And I just don't get to it. My parents get frustrated with me not using that facility – "Oh you only ever go for one night at a time." And I can only go for one or two nights at a time because I just have too much to do.

In these three cases, these coaches have embraced caring for athletes as an integral part of their role. They also care deeply about their sport and performance success, and this level of care has had consequences for their wider personal and social relationships. There can be little doubt that the world of the caring coach goes beyond the field of play and does not stop at the final whistle; indeed, Dave cares in meetings, hotels and even in players' houses. This means that coaching is an extremely demanding activity. The initial analysis in the next section, raises interesting questions about the cost paid by coaches who care for players and care about their sport.

Initial analysis by Colum Cronin

The holistic and person-centred coaching that Dave described chimed with my personal view that sport can[2] be a powerful vehicle for positive youth development (Camiré, Trudel, & Forneris, 2014; Armour, Sandford, & Duncombe, 2012; Holt, 2008; Hellison, 1995). Interestingly, Dave's positive influence on young people often occurred away from the basketball court in meetings and in discussions with athletes, teachers and family members. Indeed, Dave's story suggests that off-the-field coaching interactions are not only opportunities for Dave to listen to athletes, care for them and be a positive influence, but also productive sites in which to help improve sporting performance. For example, Dave describes how getting to know athletes away from the field of play was paramount to sporting success at a European Basketball Championship:

> On the first day we arrived at the European Championship, we sat around in a circle at the hotel, and I said, "Round one: tell each other one thing we didn't know about each other." Then I said, "Round two: now say something about you that will make someone laugh. It might make you a little bit vulnerable, but it doesn't matter; we're here together." We went around the group and told some funny stories. Then I said, "Right, round three! We are all going to share a personal battle we have had to overcome in our life." I wanted them to feel a little bit vulnerable in this moment. So I led it and gave them my story, and we went around the circle. The coaches went next, and one talked about his divorce. Then it went on to the players. The captain went first. He told us about his father passing away when he was 7 years old and how his life has been a struggle since. Another person talked about his

grandfather dying, and he's the one who would come to watch every single game. Tears were shed. Oh, a lad told us about how his brother was beating him up. He started telling us "this is why I don't like it when people shout at me." All I could think was, "Jeez if only we knew this months ago, we would have coached him differently." He's the one with the most potential, and I used to really bust his balls.

Anyway, going into the bronze medal game, which we won, we had the pre-game changing room talk. I said to them, "Lads, two weeks ago we sat in the hotel, and we talked about stuff we've overcome in our lives, challenges we've overcome." I said, "Think about those challenges. Some of you are sitting here nervous because there's a promotion game, but it's just another challenge that is nowhere near as difficult as the challenges you've had to overcome in your life. So go out there now and meet this head on like you met that challenge, and you'll walk out of here with an easy win." You could feel the energy. Everyone's sitting up straight, ready to go.

(Cronin & Armour, 2017, p. 927)

Thus, Dave's story demonstrates that coaching is a task that does not begin and end with training sessions, nor even competitions. Indeed, many researchers have recognised that coaching is a complex activity that requires greater intrapersonal insight than is often recognised (Barnson, 2014; Bowes & Jones, 2006; Cushion, 2007; Jones & Wallace, 2006; Jones, Edwards, & Tuim Viotto Filho, 2016). Dave's story builds on this body of knowledge by demonstrating how an international coach cares for athletes in private spaces such as meetings, restaurants and hotel rooms. More specifically, Dave's story illustrates how coaches can care by listening to athletes, their families and teachers. From this position (i.e. engrossed in the needs of athletes), coaches such as Dave are well placed to act in the best interests of athletes (motivational displacement).[3] Interestingly, the powerful positions of coaches enables them to enact harm and abuse (Raakman, Dorsch, & Rhind, 2010). In Dave's case, however, listening to athletes' life stories appears to have had a positive influence upon their sporting performance.[4]

It is also important to note from Dave's story that caring for the holistic development of athletes is not an easy task. Basketball coaching has clearly been an emotive and time-consuming commitment for Dave. In fact, during our interviews, when Dave explained how much he cared for players and how he addressed issues such as school behaviour and family challenges, I began to feel concern for him. He had already recounted the negative impact of coaching on his previous marriage, and the impact of the emotional and pastoral care he provided for players was evident. In fact, Dave's commitment to care for players in both school and high-performance contexts could be best described as an all-encompassing commitment. I wondered if he ever found time for rest and recuperation. I asked myself whether he was in danger of 'burning out.'

In the next two sections, we attempt to answer pressing questions about Dave's practice and the personal costs of care. From a sociological perspective, John Hayton frames care as a form of emotional labour and considers the implications for coaches such as Dave. Sören Hjälm then focuses on the issue of coach burnout and from a psychological perspective and considers whether caring in an engrossed and motivationally displaced manner can lead to burnout. Together, these perspectives provide a layered analysis of Dave's story that highlights key take-home messages for coaches concerned about the cost of care on their family and their own well-being.

Theoretical perspective 1: a sociological analysis by John Hayton. Care as an emotional labour?

Coaching and sports work is implicitly bound up with emotion (Hayton, 2017), and the care that Dave exhibits both within his professional practice and outside of his job connects with Hochschild's (1979, 2012) related concepts of emotion work and emotional labour. Emotion work or emotion management refer to the act of trying to 'feel' an emotion, to try to adjust, evoke, shape or suppress one's own feelings in line with the perceived requirements of a given social situation or context (Hochschild, 2012). Such conscious efforts made by an individual to transmute emotion by 'working on' their inner feelings to align them to situationally prescribed emotional displays is termed 'deep' acting by Hochschild (2012). There are two principal forms of deep acting as outlined by Hochschild (2012). The first is to exhort feeling, to have the will to feel and to make conscious and forced efforts to feel; however, this only allows someone to 'duck' a signal temporarily and becomes unsustainable and emotionally draining over time. The second form is to imagine feeling: to do this requires an individual to recall feelings from prior experiences and apply them in situ. In contrast to deep acting, one may also simply pretend to feel, or feign an emotion, and this is known as surface acting (Hochschild, 2012).

Hochschild (2012, p. 7) differentiates between emotion work and emotional labour, explaining that the former is undertaken within personal and private contexts, whereas as the latter is typically performed by a paid employee "to create a publicly observable facial and bodily display" that is intended to elicit a desired emotional response in their clients. Emotion work is therefore guided by 'feeling rules,' which, in turn, inform 'display rules.' Feeling rules, then, are "socially shared, often latent rules," and as such they govern how people should try to feel in a given situation (Hochschild, 1979, p. 563). For Hochschild (1979), feeling rules inform people when and how to publicly demonstrate types of emotion (display rules) appropriate to the social context.

As Hochschild (2012) expounds, maintaining an act or display of emotion which is estranged from actual feeling incurs a cumulative strain on the actor, and unless the transmutation of emotion occurs, managed feeling cannot be maintained indefinitely as emotional dissonance and emotional labour will turn to emotion fatigue, and ultimately burnout. Critically, this original framework of emotional labour did not accommodate for instances where employees may naturally or spontaneously feel what is required and expected in a specific context of paid work. To this end, Ashforth and Humphrey (1993) added a third form to the typology: 'genuine expression.' The concept of genuine expression has subsequently been appropriated within sports coaching research (c.f. Lee & Chelladurai, 2016; Lee, Chelladurai, & Kim, 2015) and has been negatively related to emotional dissonance and exhaustion.

Colum highlights Dave's love for his sport (basketball) and the care with which he expresses towards his athletes. To me, when Dave's focus is purely on the coaching of these players, he is 'being natural,' exhibiting a genuine expression which is unlikely to incur negative emotional labour. I would suggest that when Dave is fully immersed in his role, he becomes energised by it. As a case in point, Dave recounts a "pre-game changing room talk" to his players, and engrossed in this moment, he describes 'feeling the energy.' As part of this team talk, Dave explains that he "wanted them (the athletes) to feel a little bit vulnerable in this moment. So I led it, and gave them my story." Such 'expressive' emotion work is intended to serve a dual purpose according to Hochschild (1979) and Hayton (2017): to first shape Dave's own internal feelings so as to facilitate a feeling display which, in turn, is intended to elicit a desired emotional response in his athletes. My interpretation of this example is that although Dave sets out to deliver a motivational and rousing display, his feeling is in alignment with his emotion, and such congruence manifests a truly authentic display: one of passion and one of care. This, to me, is no better exemplified than by Dave's repeated use of the personal pronoun 'we,' as he becomes part of the group and part of the moment, thus evincing an expression of genuine immersion.

In contrast, however, it is other nuances of his role – some of which might not be laid out in the black and white ink of his contract – as well as aspects of his personal life, which, from my perspective, are most likely to engender emotional strain for Dave. First, Dave is regularly called upon to perform wider roles 'off the court' by both school staff and athletes' parents due to the respect and credibility he possesses across both Basketball contexts in which he operates. These role extensions take the form of 'social support' and acting as a de facto authority figure. From Dave's comments, it is apparent that he is expected to present a voice of command to the athletes in his charge. When issues to do with their schooling or home life arise, Dave is required to 'handle' the feelings of his players in order to chide them into demonstrating self-discipline and decorum within the activities in which they engage outside of basketball. To undertake such parallel roles to the business of actually coaching basketball, Dave therefore must conform to display rules that correspond to such pastoral tasks, and this may cause Dave to 'curb' feelings that are typical of his passionate and enthusiastic coaching disposition to instead present a sterner authoritarian persona in order to instil discipline. Enforcing such standards of behaviour may shift the feeling rules that Dave is accustomed to within his coaching practice and instead induce emotional labour which, over time, may lead to emotion fatigue which could spill-over into his actual coaching role.

Connectedly, and like his counterparts Julie and Jane, Dave describes his work schedule as 'crazy' and, as a consequence, the multifaceted aspects of his job reduce the time he has available for his 'home life.' This has, in the past, caused tension in his personal relationships, which would have likely aroused regular and sustained bouts of emotion work for Dave. Of his previous marriage, Dave spoke of "a constant battle every day" to try to get his ex-wife to "understand our culture" (basketball), to understand "our way of life," in the hope that he could overturn her 'hate' for (the) sport and be able see the job from his point of view. In attempting to make his marriage work and imploring his wife to understand his relationship with his job, such a challenging and protracted situation would have likely manifested in fatiguing emotion work for Dave. The key point to be made here is that the long hours and additional responsibilities generated through the combination of Dave's school-based and performance-coaching roles clearly encroach into his personal life, and when the job(s) becomes almost all consuming, it may force the coach to have to perform more emotion work within their personal life. This could potentially prove to be a vicious circle. If the home environment is similarly draining, it could lead the coach to grow increasingly estranged from those emotions that correspond to the display rules of the coaching context. On the other hand, the coaching platform could offer a cathartic escape to a highly passionate professional such as Dave, yet the trap here may be that the 'sanctuary' that becomes the workplace could draw the coach further away from their home life, thereby exacerbating private troubles.

If a coach has to labour (emotionally) on two fronts, then two critical questions emerge for me. First, does the coach, who cares 'too much' about the job take sufficient care of him or herself, and his or her own personal relationships? If the answer to the first question is 'no,' then the second question must be, at what point is the coach's capacity to care for others affected?

In sum, emotion management, whether in public (emotional labour) or in private (emotion work), is a coping mechanism that allows a person to orchestrate a countenance that is congruent with the feeling rules of the social context. However, if feeling and emotion are not regulated appropriately, then such emotional dissonance can, over time, prove detrimental to well-being and potentially lead to stress, emotional exhaustion and burnout.

Looking to solutions for those who find themselves in scenarios similar to the narrative outlined here, Dave is in the advantageous position that he is ostensibly an experienced and assured coach who is more likely than not to exhibit genuine expression through his practice. As Lee and Chelladurai (2016) reinforce, the ability to tap into the emotional labour of genuine expression is the optimal means by which to guard against emotional exhaustion. For Dave, it appears that responsibilities peripheral to his day-to-day coaching are a potential cause for overload, and the suggestion here would be for him to redefine the parameters of his role(s). For those who are not yet capable of genuine expression, instead resorting to surface acting in particular, both Hochschild (2012) and Hayton (2017) speak of emotion management 'training grounds,' such as the family, education settings, and work-related learning placements, as sites through which learners can develop their emotion coping and management strategies. Key recommendations for developing junior coaches would therefore be to a) educate them on what emotional labour is and how it might present itself in coaching episodes (Hayton, 2017) and b) to provide training opportunities/placements tied to structured supervision, mentorship and support systems (Lee & Chelladurai, 2016).

Theoretical perspective 2: a psychological analysis of burnout by Sören Hjälm

Caring and coach burnout

The description of Dave's life situation is very similar to what I (Sören) recognise from my studies in elite football (soccer) coaches in Sweden (Hjälm, Kenttä, Hassménan, & Gustafsson, 2007; Lundkvist, Gustafsson, Hjälm, & Hassmén, 2012). Through the interview, it emerges that Dave is tasked with training the players, and he is expected to assist both teachers and parents in caring for players in school as well as in their family life. Being available to care for these players means that Dave' own recovery time decreases, which in the long-term could lead to fatigue and burnout. In addition, it appears that Dave wrestles with his conscience about being unable to care for his own family, which leads to frustration. There is no doubt that Dave is exposed to a life situation that is very time-consuming and emotionally challenging. For coaches like Dave, this risks creating high levels of stress. Unfortunately, this is not uncommon in coaching.

Why are coaches stressed?

Excessive workloads and unclear roles and expectations are examples of possible risk factors for developing a high-level of burnout among coaches (Hjälmet et al., 2007; Capel, Sisley, & Desertrain, 1987). Coaches in smaller and voluntary clubs can also experience poorer working conditions compared to those coaches in elite larger clubs – e.g., part-time contracts. This can mean double work for the coach; first as a 'civilian,' coaches will work during the day, and then in the evening they will use their 'free-time' for training and matches (Hjälm et al., 2007). Many coaches who have high ambitions to lead major elite clubs work in these smaller clubs. Thus, to reach their personal goals, they may invest long working days in their own professional development. In these scenarios, it is not surprising that stress is a factor in the daily work situation of many coaches and that it may eventually lead to burn-out (Frey, 2007; Olusoga, Butt, Hays, & Maynard, 2009; Olusoga, Butt, Maynard, & Hays, 2010).

What is burnout?

Burnout is a work-related syndrome that develops over time and is characterised by fatigue, cynicism and a low sense of professional performance (Maslach, Wilmar, Schaufeli, & Leiter, 2001). Those who experience burnout may perceive a sense of being mentally and emotionally exhausted, have a negative and distant attitude to work and perceive work as less valuable or interesting. Sufferers of burnout may also experience a reduced personal ability to perform, which is characterised by impaired learning, impaired concentration ability, impaired memory capacity and feelings of low professional self-esteem (Maslach et al., 2001). Typically, it is highly motivated individuals who 'care about' improving performance in a demanding job that experience burnout. High-performance coaches like Dave fit this description. More specifically, those who suffer from burn-out have been described as very passionate, committed and moti-vated for their work (Bentzen, Lemyre, & Kenttä, 2014; Lundkvist et al., 2012). Actually, it appears that the strong internal drive in the form of devotion, which Dave exhibits, actually increases the risk of developing burnout (Pines, 1993). This is because coaches are often "passionate about what they do, but may not see the paradox of passion, which may mean that the endeavour that stimulates them most" can also cause them to burnout (Giges, Petitpas, & Vernacchia, 2004, p. 434).

What can happen to Dave in the long run? – The burnout phases

Classic burnout literature (e.g. Maslach et al., 2001) argues that burnout is a dynamic process involving several phases. In *the initial phase*, individuals often experience an inability to calm down, or to reduce their focus on their work. This description complies very well with Dave's account of his work situation. It can be described as an 'absorbent commitment' (Hallsten, 2001). As the coach has difficulty calming down, the risk is that their performance is likely to deteriorate. Deteriorating performance is also a feature of the second *depersonalisation phase* of burnout, when dramatic behavioural changes may occur. These changes are due to coaches' experience of physical and emotional fatigue. During this phase, it is common that the previously exaggerated commitment that the individual exhibited begins to change. The behavioural change usually involves individuals reducing their commitment to work by deprioritising the requirements they considered most demanding to live up to – e.g., a coach perhaps schedules fewer team meetings, or simply becomes low-key and silent in their relationship with both players and their employees. In order to avoid going further into the burnout process, the coach in the second fatigue phase, might develop a cynical approach to his surroundings and work. This cynical attitude is an unconscious coping strategy that in the short term reduces or relieves the stress the coach experiences. For example, it may feel appropriate to blame their players if the team has not performed well during a match.

In the final *burnout* phase of the process, the coach is forced to separate himself or herself from everything in the environment that creates stress for health reasons. This sometimes means that they can no longer be in touch with work colleagues, or perhaps their employer may force them on to sick leave. During this phase, the coach is unable to perform any work without having to rest. Usually, this is because the body is affected by a hormonal imbalance. The imbalance is because adrenal glands are tired of prolonged stress, resulting in constant low cortisol levels (Pruessner, Helhammer, & Kirshbaum, 1999). A person with low cortisol levels is usually very tired and stress sensitive. Depending on the duration of the individual's stress, the risk of psychosomatic diseases such as diabetes and cardiovascular disease increases (Wahlberg et al., 2009).

What does Dave need to take care of himself?

Coaches in danger of burnout or in need of care would benefit from ensuring a balance between work and recovery. Awareness about their vulnerable situation is a key precursor to action that ensures this balance. The most common prompt for individuals to start the recovery process is that they realise the seriousness of the situation they are in. This awareness can be prompted by dramatic experiences such as panic attacks or long-term and severe stress-related disease symptoms.

Once aware of their predicament, coaches can benefit from interrupting their high levels of stress. The length of the break is dependent on the person's burnout or fatigue level; the more serious the symptoms, the longer the interruption is required. However, it is not uncommon for individuals to continue as a coach for another year or more (Hjälm et al., 2007). Unfortunately, this may lead to insufficient recovery. Thus, coaches may slowly increase fatigue, which then causes them to terminate their coaching assignment due to complaints from players and management.

Through *reflection*, it is common for coaches to start re-evaluating and questioning old values and approaches, meaning that they no longer experience stress and develop strategies to handle the stress (Bernier, 1998). For example, if the coach chooses to remain as an elite coach, it is usually required that the coach changes his perception of achievement through cognitive restructuring, leading to a more relaxed attitude towards achievement. Similarly, through *reorientation* individuals can benefit from reappraising their life situation and changing their view of the future (Bernier, 1998). This means that the coach, based on what is achieved during the reflection and reorientation, might choose the option that is best for his or her health.

What can coaches do to avoid being burnout?

Many activities are available to coaches that facilitate recovery from stress. Studies that investigated the effects of recreational leisure time (evenings and weekends) show that relaxing and stimulating activities, as well as the avoidance of work-related activities, favour the recovery (Fritz & Sonnentag, 2006). Relaxing activities also have positive effects on human well-being (Fritz & Sonnentag, 2006). Examples include meditation (Grossman, Niemann, Schmidt, & Walach, 2004) yoga (Oken et al., 2004), listening to music (Pelletier, 2004), long hot baths (Bourne, 2000) progressive muscle relaxation and breathing exercises (Calder, 2003).

Different forms of physical activities such as walking, which paradoxically require some effort, have also been shown to reduce the need for recovery. This is most effective when the physical activities differ from the demands that individuals have in their daily lives, and they increase psychological well-being (endorphins) (Sonnentag, 2001; Sonnentag & Natter, 2004). Spending time in nature is also a possible source of recovery from stress (Kaplan, Kaplan, & Ryan, 1998; Stigsdotter & Grahn, 2003). In addition, it is possible that physical training involves a distraction from the surrounding demands and disturbing thoughts (Yeung, 1996; Martinsen, 2002; Jonsdottir, Rödjer, Hadzibajramovic, Börjesson, & Ahlborg Jr, 2010).

Finally, it has been argued that the most powerful mechanism to avoid burnout is to have good sleep, because it restores both biological and psychological functions in the body (Åsberg, Wahlberg, WiKlander, & Nygren, 2011; Ekstedt et al., 2006). Good sleep habits include regular awake times, appropriate durations of sleep, minimising caffeine, tobacco and alcohol intake before sleep and reducing environmental noise (Brown, Buboltz, & Soper, 2002; Brick, Seely, & Palermo, 2010). Without good sleep habits, the individual's ability to perform decreases radically and the risk of burnout increases dramatically.

How can others care for coaches?

While it is important that the coach is personally responsible for ensuring effective recovery as well as developing adequate coping strategies, it is equally important to eliminate the stressful factors that arise in the work situation. In order to avoid the coach experiencing excessive workload and high demands, the organisational leadership should be clear when describing the coach's role, duties and responsibilities. For examples, clubs employing young coaches with relatively little or poor professional experience of the elite environment should pay particular attention to the early signs of stress symptoms. This is because it appears that young trainers with less experience are at greater risk of burnout (Gencay & Gencay, 2011). It is also important to point out that clubs, as employers, have responsibilities and a duty of care to their employees.

Implications from Dave's story

Dave's story suggests that caring for athletes is not an easy task. On the contrary, it is emotive, time consuming and laborious. It is, however, rewarding, and for Dave, it is very much a part of his identity and his everyday life. This means that Dave's passion for sport and care for players, can negatively affect his relationships with family and friends. In Dave's case, it has been a struggle for him to meet the demands of his coaching and fulfil the expectations of family members. I suspect that this is not an uncommon experience amongst coaches. It is also a problematic situation because, as John explains, caring for athletes can be an emotionally straining process. This is because coaches may need to present certain emotional dispositions in order to care for athletes – e.g., supportive and optimistic language. This is not to say that coaches are not authentic in their care, but rather to care appropriately, coaches may need to manage their emotions. This can be a fatiguing process. Of course, coaches may suffer more 'emotional fatigue' if they also have to manage emotions in their own personal lives. Interestingly, as Sören describes, when the (emotional) demands placed upon coaches consistently exceed the resources that they have, then coaches are liable to experience burnout. Burnout is a process, which can have negative consequences for the health and performance of coaches (McNeill, Durand-Bush, & Lemyre, 2016). Thus, Dave's story and the accompanying analyses raise important questions to consider. Specifically:

- Coach researchers need to further explore the role of emotion in coaching. What are the emotional demands of coaching? Do these demands differ depending on the environment and athletes that coaches' experience? This is an important question, because if coaching is to be recognised as a caring activity, then coaches will be required to emotionally engage with athletes.

- Coach educators also have a responsibility to consider emotions and coaching. How do they prepare coaches to enact emotional labour? Can this emotional labour be developed? Are coach educators aware of what emotional labour is required and undertaken by coaches?

- In addition to understanding the emotional role in coaching, it is also important that coaching researchers further explore burnout. How should existing coaches prevent burnout? How do coaches recover from burnout? Can coaches 'self-care'? These questions have been somewhat addressed earlier, but coaches' accounts of burnout are rare and more case studies are desirable (McNeill et al., 2016; Hjälm et al., 2007). Large-scale intervention studies that address coach burnout are also required (Lyle, 2018).

- Coach educators could, perhaps, be positive influences who prepare coaches to manage their emotional fatigue. Furthermore, recovering from burnout is preceded by an awareness of one's fatigue. Do coach educators help coaches to recognise the signs and symptoms of burnout? Could coach educators care for coaches in this manner? Could they educate coaches to self-care?

- Finally, burnout is linked to a deficit of resources and capacity to respond to demands. To date, most solutions to burnout have focused on the individual (Kilo & Hassmén, 2016). As Sören alludes to, however, coach employers such as a sport clubs and national governing bodies also have a duty of care towards coaches. Indeed, research suggests that when organisations provide supportive environments, coaches are less likely to experience burnout (Kilo & Hassmén, 2016). Such environments could be characterised as stable and collaborative contexts with a realistic/sustainable approach to coaches' remuneration and ensuring that coaches are valued and rewarded. Thus, employing organisations have an important role in developing caring contexts for coaches.

Notes

1 This reflects the amateur status of much basketball coaching in the UK. Although played extensively in schools, professional and elite structures in the UK remain underdeveloped.

2 However, I also recognise that sport can be a negative experience for many people.
3 See Chapter 2 for further discussion of the terms engrossment, and motivational displacement.
4 Readers should be cautious in extrapolating these behaviours to their own contexts and may want to consider the efficacy and ethical aspects of this behaviour.

Bibliography

Armour, K., Sandford, R., & Duncombe, R. (2012). Positive youth development and physical activity/sport interventions: Mechanisms leading to sustained impact. *Physical Education and Spot Pedagogy, 18*(3), 256–281. doi:10.1080/17408989.2012.666791

Åsberg, M., Wahlberg, K., WiKlander, M., & Nygren, Å. (2011). Psykiskt sjuk av stress: Diagnostik, patofysiologi och rehabilitering. *Lakartidningen, 108*(36), 1680–1683.

Ashforth, B. E., & Humphrey, R. H. (1993). Emotional labor in service roles: The influence of identity. *Academy of Management Review, 18*(1), 88–115. doi:10.5465/amr.1993.3997508

Barnson, S. C. (2014). Toward a theory of coaching paradox. *Quest, 66*(4), 371–384. doi:10.1080/00336297.2014.918891

Bentzen, M., Lemyre, P.-N., & Kenttä, G. (2014). The process of burnout among professional sport coaches through the lens of self-determination theory: A qualitative approach. *Sports Coaching Review, 3*(2), 101–116. doi:10.1080/2164062.2015.1035050

Bernier, D. (1998). A study of coping: Successful recovery from severe burnout and other reactions to severe work-related stress. *Work & Stress, 12*(1), 50–65. doi:10.1080/02678379808256848

Bourne, E. J. (2000). *The anxiety and phobia workbook.* Oakland, CA: New Harbinger.

Bowes, I., & Jones, R. L. (2006). Working at the edge of chaos: Understanding coaching as a complex, interpersonal system. *The Sport Psychologist, 20*(2), 235–245.

Brick, C. A., Seely, D. L., & Palermo, T. M. (2010). Association between sleep hygiene and sleep quality in medical students. *Behavioural Sleep Medicine, 8*(2), 113–121. doi:10.1080/15402001003622925

Brown, F. C., Buboltz, W. C., & Soper, B. (2002). Relationship of sleep hygiene awareness, sleep hygiene practices, and sleep quality in University students. *Behavioural Medicine, 28*(1), 33–38. doi:10.1080/0896 4280209596396

Calder, A. (2003, September 1–August). Recovery strategies for sports performance. *USOC Olympic Coach E-Magazine.* Retrieved from http://coachingusolympicteam.com

Camiré, M., Trudel, P., & Forneris, T. (2014). Examining how model youth sport coaches learn to facilitate positive youth development. *Physical Education and Sport Pedagogy*, *19*(1), 1–17. doi:10.1080/17408989.2012.726975

Capel, S. A., Sisley, B. L., & Desertrain, G. S. (1987). The relationship of role conflict and role ambiguity to burnout in high school basketball coaches. *Journal of Sport Psychology*, *9*(2), 106–117. doi:10.1123/jsp.9.2.106

Côté, J., Young, B., North, J., & Duffy, P. (2007). Towards a definition of excellence in sport coaching. *International Journal of Coaching Science*, *1*(1), 3–17.

Cronin, C., & Armour, K. M. (2017). 'Being' in the coaching world: New insights on youth performance coaching from an interpretative phenomenological approach. *Sport, Education and Society*, *22*(8), 919–931. doi: 10.1080/13573322.2015.1108912

Cushion, C. J. (2007). Modelling the complexity of the coaching process. *International Journal of Sports Science & Coaching*, *2*(4), 395–401.

Department for Education. (2013). *National curriculum in England: PE programmes of study*. London: Department of Education.

Ekstedt, M., Söderström, M., Åkerstedt, T., Nilsson, J., Søndergaard, H. P., & Aleksander, P. (2006). Disturbed sleep and fatigue in occupational burnout. *Scandinavian Journal of Work, Environment & Health*, *32*, 121–131.

Frey, M. (2007). College coaches' experiences with stress: 'Problem solvers' have problems, too. *The Sport Psychologist*, *21*(1), 38–57. doi:10.1123/tsp.21.1.38

Fritz, C., & Sonnentag, S. (2006). Recovery, well-being, and performance-related outcomes: The role of workload and vacation experiences. *Journal of Applied Psychology*, *91*(4), 936–945. doi:10.1037/0021-9010.91.4.936

Gencay, S., & Gencay, O. A. (2011). Burnout among judo coaches in Turkey. *Journal of Occupational Health*, *53*(5), 365–370. doi:10.1539/joh.10-0064-FS

Giges, B., Petitpas, A. J., & Vernacchia, R. A. (2004). Helping coaches meet their own needs: Challenges for the sport psychology consultant. *The Sport Psychologist*, *18*, 430–444. doi:10.1123/tsp.18.4.430

Grossman, P., Niemann, L., Schmidt, S., & Walach, H. (2004). Mindfulness-based stress reduction and health benefits: A meta-analysis. *Journal of Psychosomatic Research*, *57*(1), 35–43. doi:10.1016/S0022-3999(03)00573-7

Hallsten, L. (2001). Utbränning. En processmodell. *Svensk rehabilitering*, *3*, 26–35.

Hayton, J. (2017). 'They need to learn to take it on the chin': Exploring the emotional labour of student volunteers in a a sports-based outreach project in the North East of England. *Sociology of Sport Journal*, *34*(2), 136–147. doi:10.1123/ssj.2016-0098

122   *Colum Cronin et al.*

Hellison, D. (1995). *Teaching responsibility through physical activity.* Champaign, IL: Human Kinetics.

Hjälm, S., Kenttä, G., Hassménan, P., & Gustafsson, H. (2007). Burnout among elite soccer coaches. *Journal of Sport Behavior, 30*(4), 415–427.

Hochschild, A. R. (1979). Emotion work, feeing rules, and social structure. *American Journal of Sociology, 85*(3), 551–575. doi:10.1086/227049

Hochschild, A. R. (2012). *The managed heart: Commercialisation of human feeling.* Berkeley, CA: University of California Press.

Holt, N. (2008). *Positive youth development through sport.* London: Routledge.

Jones, R. L., Edwards, C., & Tuim Viotto Filho, I. A. (2016). Activity theory, complexity and sports coaching: An epistemology for a discipline. *Sport, Education and Society, 21*(2), 200–216. doi:10.1080/13573322.2014.895713

Jones, R. L., & Wallace, M. (2006). The coach as 'orchestrator': More realistically managing the complex coaching context. In R. L. Jones (Ed.), *The sports coach as educator: Re-conceptualising sports coaching* (pp. 51–64). London: Routledge.

Jonsdottir, I. H., Rödjer, L., Hadzibajramovic, E., Börjesson, M., & Ahlborg Jr, G. (2010). A prospective study of leisure-time physical activity and mental health in Swedish health care workers and social insurance officers. *Preventive Medicine, 51*(5), 373–377. doi:10.1016/j.ypmed.2010.07.019

Kaplan, R., Kaplan, S., & Ryan, S. L. (1998). *With people in mind: Design, and management of everyday nature.* Washington, DC: Island Press.

Kilo, R. A., & Hassmén, P. (2016). Burnout and turnover intentions in Australian coaches as related to organisational support and perceived control. *Original Research, 11*(2), 151–161. doi:10.1177/1747954116636710

Lee, Y. H., & Chelladurai, P. (2016). Affectivity, emotional labor, emotional exhaustion, and emotional intelligence in coaching. *Journal of Applied Sport Psychology, 28*(2), 170–184. doi:10.1080/10413200.2015.1092481

Lee, Y. H., Chelladurai, P., & Kim, Y. (2015). Emotional labor in sports coaching: Development of a model. *Journal of Sports Science & Coaching, 10*(2–3), 561–575. doi:10.1260/1747-9541.10.2–3.561

Lundkvist, E., Gustafsson, H., Hjälm, S., & Hassmén, P. (2012). An interpretative phenomenological analysis of burnout and recovery in elite soccer coaches. *Qualitative Research in Sport, Exercise and Health, 4,* 400–419. doi:10.1080/2159676X.2012.693526

Lyle, J. (2018). The transferability of sport coaching research: A critical commentary. *Quest,* 1–9. doi:10.1080/00336297.2018.1453846

Martinsen, E. W. (2002). Fysisk aktivitet – medisin mot utbrändhet? In A. Roness, & S. B. Mattiesen, *Utbrent, Krevende jobber – gode liv?* Oslo: Fagbokforlaget.

Maslach, C., Wilmar, B., Schaufeli, W. B., & Leiter, M. P. (2001). Job burnout. *Annual Review of Psychology, 52,* 397–422. doi:10.1146/annurev.psych.52.1.397

McNeill, K., Durand-Bush, N., & Lemyre, P. (2016). Understanding coach burnout and underlying. *Sports Coaching Review*, 179–196. doi:10.1080/21640629.2016.1163008

Oken, B. S., Kishiyama, S., Zajdel, D., Bourdette, D., Carlsen, J., Haas, M., . . . Mass, M. (2004). Randomized controlled trial of yoga and exercise in multiple sclerosis. *Neurology*, *62*(11), 2058–2064. doi:10.1212/01.WNL.0000129534.88602.5C

Olusoga, P., Butt, J., Hays, K., & Maynard, I. (2009). Stress in elite sports coaching: Identifying stressors. *Journal of Applied Sport Psychology*, *21*(4), 442–459. doi:10.1080/10413200903222921

Olusoga, P., Butt, J., Maynard, I., & Hays, K. (2010). Stress and coping: A study of world class coaches. *Journal of Applied Sport Psychology*, *22*(3), 274–293. doi:10.1080/10413201003760968

Pelletier, C. L. (2004). The effect of music on decreasing arousal due to stress: A meta-analysis. *Journal of Music Therapy*, *41*(3), 192–214. doi:10.1093/jmt/41.3.192

Pines, A. M. (1993). Burnout an existential perspectives. In W. B. Schaufeli, C. Maslach, & T. Marek (Eds.), *Professional burnout: Recent developments in theory and research* (pp. 19–32). Washington, DC: Taylor and Francis.

Pruessner, J. C., Helhammer, D. H., & Kirshbaum, C. (1999). Burnout, perceived stress, and cortisol responses to awakening. *Psychosomatic Medicine*, *61*(2), 197–204.

Raakman, E., Dorsch, K., & Rhind, D. (2010). The development of a typology of abusive coaching behaviours within youth sport. *International Journal of Sports Science & Coaching*, *5*(4), 503–515. doi:10.1260/1747-9541.5.4.503

Sonnentag, S. (2001). Work, recovery activities, and individual well-being: A diary study. *Journal of Occupational Health Psychology*, *6*(3), 196–210. doi:10.1037/1076-8998.6.3.196

Sonnentag, S., & Natter, E. (2004). Flight attendants' daily recovery from work: Is there no place like home? *International Journal of Stress Management*, *11*(4), 366–391. doi:10.1037/1072-5245.11.4.366

Stigsdotter, U., & Grahn, P. (2003). Experiencing a garden: A healing garden for people suffering from burnout diseases. *Journal of Therapeutic Horticulture*, *14*(5), 38–48.

Wahlberg, K., Ghatan, P. H., Modell, S., Nygren, Å., Ingvar, M., Åsberg, M., & Heilig, M. (2009). Suppressed neuroendocrine stress response in depressed women on job-stress-related long-term sick leave: A stable marker potentially suggestive of preexisting vulnerability. *Biological Psychiatry*, *65*(9), 742–747. doi:10.1016/j.biopsych.2008.10.035

Yeung, R. R. (1996). The acute effects of exercise on mood state. *Journal of Psychosomatic Research*, *40*(2), 123–141. doi:10.1016/0022-3999(95)00554-4

8 Conclusions, guidelines and future questions

Colum Cronin and Kathleen Armour

To our knowledge, this is the first academic book that is wholly devoted to examining care in sport coaching. The book is, therefore, able to make a significant contribution to the field by drawing attention to this pertinent, yet under explored issue. As authors, however, we wanted to go beyond highlighting; we wanted to analyse the place of care in coaching in a rigorous and critical manner. Rigour is designed into this book through the adoption of a phenomenological methodology to explore care in the case studies, and this is explained in detail in Chapter 3. Using phenomenology helped to ensure that our theoretical observations of care are derived from systematic analysis of coaches' lived experiences. Criticality is evident throughout the book, for example in Chapter 2, where Noddings care theory is critiqued, and in Chapter 7, where the negative implications of caring are considered.

Taking a rigorous and critical approach to care is important because care in coaching is acknowledged as something that happens and is often present, but at the same time seems to happen 'under the radar' of analyses of coaching practice. This is remiss because 'duty of care' has become synonymous with minimum standards of child protection and, is a key part of procedures such as risk assessment. Yet at times, these processes appear to be grounded in the need to avoid litigation rather than a genuine concern for athlete welfare (Harthill & Lang, 2014). The challenge for this book was to take the debate forward and to advocate for a relational approach to care built upon concepts such as engrossment, motivational displacement and reciprocity. As a result, we go beyond drawing attention to uncaring acts in sport. Rather, we aim to make a new contribution to the literature that can prompt readers to reflect on key relationships in coaching by providing rich examples of care processes in the lived experiences of real coaches.

Reflecting our own pedagogical identities, we also sought to ensure that the book could contribute to coach learning. To that end, we utilised the pedagogical cases concept (Armour, 2014) as a bridge between care theory, disciplinary evidence and coaches' lives. Specifically, Chapters 4–7 provided grounded accounts of coaching practices. In these case studies, practical accounts of everyday coaching are narrated, and these provide readers with contextually situated descriptions of care experiences. Within each chapter, two analyses from different disciplinary perspectives accompany the narratives. In these sections, a range of authors use a variety of disciplinary lenses to consider how coaches might better care for athletes and themselves. This approach reflects our aspiration to produce a resource that can prompt practitioners to learn about care and improve their practice.

With the aspiration to inform coach learning and practice in mind, this chapter reinforces and clarifies the key lessons learnt from earlier sections. To that end, we have identified eight conclusions about care in sport coaching. These conclusions will be of interest to coaches, coach educators, policy makers and researchers and may serve as an 'aide-memoire' for readers. Following, these conclusions, a brief and tentative series of 'good practice' guidelines are presented. The guidelines are derived from the grounded accounts of care that have been presented in the four pedagogical cases (Chapters 4–7). The guidelines are designed to be of value to coach educators who develop courses, resources and workshops. They can also be of value to coaches who seek to improve their everyday practice. Finally, the chapter concludes with some future considerations. Through these considerations, we acknowledge that while the book makes a new contribution to coaching theory and practice, it is, however, the start of a conversation, rather than the end.

Eight key conclusions

Conclusion 1: coach–athlete relationships should be caring relationships

As the book proceeds from theory (Chapter 2) and on to the pedagogical cases (Chapter 4–7), a picture emerges of care as a relational and dialogical concept. For example, Dave's athletes share their challenging social issues with him through intimate group discussions (Chapter 7). Similarly, Jane's athletes turn to her for emotional support because they have a long-term relationship with her. For Noddings, who has extensively studied caring practice (Noddings, 1988, 1999, 2013), a relational notion of care is not a new concept (see Chapter 2 for further details). Yet, to date, few coaching researchers have explicitly recognised coaching as a caring relationship. This is surprising because most governing bodies accept that coaches have a duty of care, and there is a substantial body of literature that argues that coaching is essentially a relational activity (Jones & Wallace, 2006; Jones, Potrac, Cushion, Ronglan, & Davey, 2011; Jowett & Poczwardowski, 2006; Potrac & Jones, 2009). Accordingly, it is reasonable to conclude, as this book does, that it is within coach–athlete relationships that coaches should exercise their 'duty of care.' Thus, how coaches care should not be limited to basic safeguarding procedures such as risk assessments. Rather coaches should also enact their duty of care through social interaction, dialogue and emotional exchange with athletes. This conclusion has significant implications because it 1) prompts coaches to reconsider their relationships as caring relationships, 2) prompts coach educators to consider whether they adequately address care within their formal curricula and courses and 3) prompts researchers to reconsider their methods when studying coaching practices.

Conclusion 2: a care paradox may exist in coaching

Given the limited research on care in coaching, readers may conclude that there is an absence of care in coaching. We do not subscribe to this view. For example, many coaches care in a virtuous sense (Noddings, 2007) in that they 'carefully plan' sessions and 'take care' when deciding tactics. Additionally, many coaches 'care about' winning, 'care about' their supporters, 'care about' fellow coaches and 'care about' their sports in general. We also predict, based upon positive youth development literature (e.g. Armour, 2014; Camiré, Trudel, & Forneris, 2014; Fry, 2010), that many coaches care for players in a way, which is affective, committed and in the best interests of the players. Paradoxically, however, regular accounts of abusive and uncaring coaching practice are reported. These are often high profile and can involve sexual, emotional, physical harm and neglect (Raakman, Dorsch, & Rhind, 2010). Unfortunately, these incidents have been reported in many international contexts (Lang & Harthill, 2015). With these reports in mind, we conclude that although care is *implicit* in many coaches' everyday lives, it needs to become *explicitly* present in all. To that end, care in coaching should no longer be 'taken for granted' or 'go without saying.' On the contrary, in order to help individuals flourish, caring relationships that are reciprocal and dialogical should be at the forefront of coaching practices, coach education provision, and coaching policies.

Conclusion 3: caring relationships are dynamic and complex

As evident across the four case studies, coaches can engage in caring relationships that are reciprocal and serve the best interests of athletes. In these relationships, the athlete's voice is present, and this means that athletes can 1) inform how coaches care, 2) acknowledge the care that coaches provide and 3) receive the care in ways that meet their needs. The reciprocal nature of these relationships does mean, however, that caring relationships are complex. For example, how coaches care for athletes must vary depending on the needs and desires of the individual athlete. In Chapter 5, for example, Terry illustrated how he empowered experienced athletes to self-care and exercise autonomous decision as they approached retirement. Conversely, in Chapter 4, Jane cared for her younger athletes by monitoring them at social events where alcohol was consumed. Thus, a "one-size-fits-all" approach to care is unlikely to meet the needs of individual athletes. Moreover, as athletes develop, so too must the caring relationship between coaches and athletes. Thus, caring relationships will always be fluid and dynamic.

Conclusion 4: caring as a situated act

In Chapter 2, the notion of a caring climate was introduced (Gano-Overway, 2014). The 'caring climate' concept asserts that caring relationships are not confined to the 'carer' and 'cared for.' Rather, when coaches exhibit caring dispositions (empathy, authentic listening, serving the needs of others), they can contribute to a wider climate wherein other individuals, such as athletes and fellow staff, may reinforce caring behaviours (Fry, 2010). This is an important point because it acknowledges that caring dyads are situated in wider contexts. The case studies within this book (Chapter 4–7) extend this insight by illustrating that not only can coaches influence a wider caring climate but also, reflexively, a wider climate can influence how coaches care. For example, in Chapter 4, Jane illustrates how off the field environments such as hotels and social events, provide opportunities for dialogue with athletes. Terry (Chapter 5), describes how technology enables him to care for athletes' health. In Chapter 6, Jane provides examples of how other individuals such as team captains and medical staff can support her attempts to care. Conversely, Dave's story illustrates how time-consuming and intense environments can hamper a coach's capacity to care. These examples illustrate that the environment, context and the network of individuals that coaches encounter influence care. Thus, care needs to be viewed as a situated act, and this has implications for those involved in coaching such as athletes, parents, organisations and governing bodies.

Conclusion 5: reappraising nurturing care

As mentioned earlier, accounts of good care are rare in coaching literature. Conversely, stereotypical caricatures of aggressive, 'macho' and highly vocal coaches are plentiful in media portrayals of coaching. The case studies in this book, however, demonstrate that some coaches engage in nurturing care. This includes demonstrating empathy and engaging in authentic dialogue through an emphasis on listening. Terry (Chapter 6), for instance, is keen to listen to his athletes and wants them to explain how performances *feel*. Jane (Chapter 4) provides 'chocolate milk' for her athletes when they finish races. For us as authors, we came to understand that listening, empathy and nurturing care are valuable behaviours that are perhaps not recognised enough in the existing coaching literature. For example, a large body of coach behaviour literature quantifies coaches' instructional behaviours but does not assess their listening capacity at all (Cope, Partington, & Harvey, 2017; Cushion, Harvey, Muir, & Nelson, 2012; Erickson, Côté, Hollenstein, & Deakin, 2011; Lacy & Darst, 1984).

Interestingly, we notice from our case studies that empathy and dialogue often occur in off the field environments, which could be described as 'backstage' contexts (Jones et al., 2011; Cronin & Armour, 2017). For example, Jane uses online technology to connect with athletes from home, while Dave occasionally has dinner with athletes and their families. We speculate that this off-the-field care is perhaps under recognised. Moreover, because much caring work is hidden from public view, it may also be undervalued (Lynch, 2010). This is an important observation, because Jane asserts that in elite sport there may be a 'care ceiling,' above which care is not valued or appreciated (Grummell, Devine, & Lynch, 2009). Thus, for coaches, care remains an essential, though largely hidden and perhaps under-appreciated, part of their everyday practice.

Conclusion 7: extending nurturing care with rules-based considerations

Although nurturing and dialogical care were present in all four case studies, there were instances where the coaches cared in ways that are different to the maternal approach advocated by Noddings (2013). In particular, Terry (Chapter 5) utilised technology and scientifically informed work–rest ratios to protect and care for athletes. This is a 'rules-based' form of care, and Noddings has been sceptical of such approaches (Noddings, 1984). Noddings early work and that of Carol Gilligan (Gilligan, 1982) argued that rules-based approaches to social justice may be normative, but they are not neutral. This is because scientifically informed rules, standards and practices are socially determined and enforced. On this premise, Noddings and Gilligan were mindful that rules-based approaches may disproportionally undervalue actions such as care, which are hard to quantify and may be less valued because they are associated with feminine labour.

Supporting Noddings' assertions, a small corpus of research in sport has identified how the implementation of rules-based sport science can be dehumanising to athletes who may feel as though they are merely "cogs in a machine" (e.g. Williams & Manley, 2016). Recently, Cronin, Whitehead, Webster and Huntley (2017) argue that this occurs because the development and utilisation of technology happens without due concern for care and athletes. In contrast, however, Terry utilises technology as a means to care for athletes' health. Indeed, he couples scientific information with genuine dialogue and concern for athletes. This approach illustrates that within a coaching setting, technology can be developed to facilitate care and can be a prompt for a more human focused coaching approach. Therefore, coaches should not conceive of nurturing care as the antithesis of scientific or research informed practice. Rather, coaches can use technology and science, *in conjunction* with caring dispositions, as a means of helping athletes to flourish.

Conclusion 8: learning how to care for others and for ourselves

Many of us will have benefitted from care provided by parents and guardians, wider family, teachers, mentors and of course sport coaches. This does not mean, however, that we have all learnt how to care appropriately from these role models. Furthermore, given that care in sport coaching is dynamic (conclusion 3) and situated (conclusion 4), learning how to care is a complex task. Indeed, the complexity is more apparent if we consider the reflexive influence that others can have, both as barriers and as enablers, on our capacity to care. Thus, if we are to establish care through explicit and intentional relationships, coaches will need to learn how to support athletes, connect with athletes, empower athletes, nurture care in athletes and establish safe 'care full' environments (Gano-Overway & Guivernau, in press). As Chapter 7 demonstrates, coaches also need to learn to self-care. Thus, it is incumbent on coach researchers, educators and policy makers to develop new resources, activities and systems that can help coaches learn how to care for others and themselves.

Guidelines – what lessons can coaches take from the case studies?

The pedagogical cases within this book suggest the following:

1 Coaches should consider caring relationships as an essential part of their practice. Caring relationships should, therefore, not be taken for granted or allowed to go unremarked 'under the radar,' but instead should be explicitly planned for, delivered and reviewed.
2 Listening, observing and empathising are useful behaviours for coaches because these dispositions help coaches to understand their athletes' needs (engrossment).

3 Understanding athletes' needs is a precursor to caring for athletes (motivational displacement) and thus should be a key concern at the outset of coach–athlete relationships.

4 By engaging athletes in dialogue and genuinely listening to their voices, coaches can ensure their care is acknowledged, appreciated and received.

5 Coaches should consider utilising off the field environments such as hotels and training grounds to care for athletes. These environments might be conducive to authentic dialogue.

6 Technology and scientific knowledge can be effective aids to caring. Coaches should, however, use these aids alongside authentic dialogue and as a means of helping individuals to flourish.

7 In order to help athletes flourish, coaches can contribute to the development of caring climates. Exhibiting careful acts and valuing care can prompt others such as parents, fellow staff, athletes and employers to engage in caring.

8 With the notion of a care full climate in mind, coaches should be aware of the limitations of their expertise. In particular, coaches may need to draw upon – for example – medical professionals, welfare officers, sport scientists or other coaches to ensure that the needs of athletes are met.

9 Self-care is important when it comes to coaching because coaches may experience high demands on their labour. Indeed, caring for others may be a laborious act and thus coaches should be mindful of their own care needs.

10 Coaches can self-care by ensuring they have adequate rest and resources to complete their work. Moreover, they have a self-care duty to set aside time and space for recovery and relaxation.

Final thoughts: how can research support practitioners, educators and employers?

In addressing the issue of care in coaching, this book has identified implications for both coaches and other individuals. For example, coach educators, may need to consider how they prepare coaches to care. Employers and governing bodies may need to consider how they assess and develop caring practice. It would be helpful, therefore, if more and more appropriate research was available to support the care process. The question is, What would such a research agenda look like?

To begin with, we suggest that there is a need for the development of a whole range of complex case studies that explore the experiences of 'cared for' individuals – i.e., the athletes themselves. We need to hear how athletes experience care in order to further problematise coaching as a caring activity. It is also important to ensure that cases are drawn from the lived experiences of athletes and coaches such that care is understood in an emancipatory framework rather than as an overbearing and potentially oppressive act. Case studies could also further our understanding of caring in specific circumstances, given that contextual specificity is a key feature of the case study method. Examples include how best should coaches care for athletes with mental health concerns? How best should coaches care for athletes who experience failure? How best should coaches care for athletes who move closer to retirement? Such case studies would be of immense value to coaches, coach educators and policy makers because narrative cases resonate with learners and help them to 'see' alignments and misalignments between the case and their own circumstances. Following on from this work, researchers also need to explore alternative models of care such as a virtue theory approach and concepts such as the care ceiling. This theorisation of care will help to provide alternative insights that connect care theory with the lived experiences of coaches. Researchers may also look to alternative occupations and professions, for example, nursing, to gain additional insights into care. Indeed, there is no reason why best practice from such fields could not inform future sport and physical activity policy.

As this book illustrates, research that connects theory and practice is a useful learning and professional development tool that may ultimately benefit athletes, coaches and the sport itself. In this book, we have argued that it is essential for all parties involved in sport coaching to understand and implement best caring practice. After all, coaching is, first and foremost, about helping individuals flourish.

Bibliography

Armour, K. (2014). *Pedagogical cases in physical education and youth sport* (1st ed.). Oxon: Routledge.

Armour, K., Sandford, R., & Duncombe, R. (2012). Positive youth development and physical activity/sport interventions: Mechanisms leading to sustained impact. *Physical Education and Sport Pedagogy, 18*(3), 256–281. doi:10.1080/17408989.2012.666791

Camiré, M., Trudel, P., & Forneris, T. (2014). Examining how model youth sport coaches learn to facilitate positive youth development. *Physical Education and Sport Pedagogy, 19*(1), 1–17. doi:10.1080/17408989.20 12.726975

Cope, E., Partington, M., & Harvey, S. (2017). A review of the use of a systematic observation method in coaching research between 1997 and 2016. *Journal of Sports Sciences, 35*(20), 2042–2050. doi:10.1080/0264 0414.2016.1252463

Cronin, C., & Armour, K. M. (2017). 'Being' in the coaching world: New insights on youth performance coaching from an interpretative phenomenological approach. *Sport, Education and Society, 22*(8), 919–931. doi:10. 1080/13573322.2015.1108912

Cronin, C., Whitehead, A. E., Webster, S., & Huntley, T. (2017). Transforming, storing and consuming athletic experiences: A coach's narrative of using a video application. *Sport, Education and Society*, 1–13. doi:10.108 0/13573322.2017.1355784

Cushion, C., Harvey, S., Muir, B., & Nelson, L. (2012). Developing the Coach Analysis and Intervention System (CAIS): Establishing validity and reliability of a computerised systematic observation instrument. *Journal of Sports Sciences, 30*(2), 203–218. doi:10.1080/02640414.201 1.635310

Erickson, K., Côté, J., Hollenstein, T., & Deakin, J. (2011). Examining coach-athlete interactions using state space grids: An observational analysis in competitive youth sport. *Psychology of Sport and Exercise, 12*(6), 645–654. doi:10.1016/j.psychsport.2011.06.006

Fry, M. D. (2010). Creating a positive climate for young athletes from day 1. *Journal of Sport Psychology in Action, 1*(1), 33–41. doi:10.1080/21520 704.2010.518224

Gano-Overway, L. A. (2014). The caring climate: How sport environments can develop empathy in young people. In K. Pavlovich, & K. Krahnke (Eds.), *Organising through empathy* (pp. 166–183). New York, NY: Routledge.

Gano-Overway, L. A., & Guivernau, M. (in press). Setting the SCENE: Developing a caring youth sport environment. *Journal of Sport Psychology in Action*. doi:10.1080/21520704.2017.1343214

Gilligan, C. (1982). *In a different voice*. Boston, MA: Harvard.

Grummell, B., Devine, D., & Lynch, K. (2009). The care-less manager: Gender, care and new managerialism in higher education. *Gender and Education, 21*(2), 191–208. doi:10.1080/09540250802392273

Harthill, M., & Lang, M. (2014). 'I know people think I'm a complete pain in the neck': An examination of the introduction of child protection and 'safeguarding' in English sport from the perspective of national governing body safeguarding lead officers. *Social Sciences, 3*(4), 606–627. doi:10.3390/socsci3040606

Jones, R. L., Potrac, P., Cushion, C., Ronglan, L., & Davey, C. (2011). Erving Goffman: Interaction and impression management, playing the coaching role. In R. Jones, P. Potrac, C. Cushion, & L. Ronglan, *The sociology of sports coaching* (pp. 15–27). London: Routledge.

Jones, R. L., & Wallace, M. (2006). The coach as 'orchestrator': More realistically managing the complex coaching context. In R. L. Jones (Ed.), *The sports coach as educator: Re-conceptualising sports coaching* (pp. 51–64). London: Routledge.

Jowett, S., & Poczwardowski, A. (2006). Critical issues in the conceptualization of and future research on coach-athlete relationship. In S. Jowett, & D. Lavalee (Eds.), *Social psychology in sport* (pp. 69–81). Champaign, IL: Human Kinetics.

Lacy, A. C., & Darst, P. W. (1984). Evolution of a systematic observation system: The ASU coaching observation instrument. *Journal of Teaching in Physical Education, 3*(3), 59–66. doi:10.1123/jtpe.3.3.59

Lang, M., & Harthill, M. (2015). *Safeguarding, child protection and abuse in sport: International perspectives in research, policy and practice.* London: Routledge.

Lynch, K. (2010). Carelessness: A hidden doxa of higher education. *Arts and Humanities in Higher Education, 9*(1), 54–67. doi:10.1177/147402 2209350104

Noddings, N. (1984). *Caring: A feminine approach to ethics and moral education.* Berkeley, CA: University of California Press.

Noddings, N. (1988). An ethic of caring and its implications for instructional arrangements. *American Journal of Education, 96*(2), 215–230. doi:10.1086/443894

Noddings, N. (1999). Response: Two concepts of caring. In R. Curren (Ed.), *Philosophy of education* (pp. 36–39). Champaign, IL: Philosophy of Education Society.

Noddings, N. (2007). Caring as relation and virtue in teaching. In R. L. Walker, & P. J. Ivanhoe (Eds.), *Working virtue: Virtue ethics and contemporary moral problems* (pp. 41–60). Oxford: Oxford University Press.

Noddings, N. (2013). *Caring: A relational approach to ethics and moral education* (2nd ed.). London: University of California Press.

Potrac, P., & Jones, R. (2009). Power, conflict and cooperation: Toward a micropolitics of coaching. *Quest, 61*(2), 223–236. doi:10.1080/0033629 7.2009.10483612

Raakman, E., Dorsch, K., & Rhind, D. (2010). The development of a typology of abusive coaching behaviours within youth sport. *International Journal of Sports Science & Coaching, 5*(4), 503–515. doi:10.1260/1747-9541.5.4.503

Williams, S., & Manley, A. (2016). Elite coaching and the technocratic engineer: Thanking the boys at Microsoft! *Sport, Education and Society, 21*(6), 828–850. doi:10.1080/13573322.2014.958816

Index

3C+1 coach-athlete relationship
   model 5–6

abuse or neglect, dealing with 90
abusive behaviours, typology of 6
abusive coaching practice 1, 5,
   126–127
athletes: autonomy of 62, 70, 74–77;
   dehumanising 70, 74; empowering
   67–68; knowing and involving
   in coaching 58; maturation and
   development of 85–86
authentic dialogue 52, 53
autonomy and care 62, 70, 74–77

Ball, Arnetha 32
basketball, amateur status of 119n1
Battistich, Victor 21–22
best practice guidelines 130–131
biographies: Dave 103–107; Jane
   46–48; Julie 82; Terry 64
burnout: avoiding 117; Dave and
   113–114; defined 114–115; duty
   of care towards coaches and 119;
   phases of 115–116; self-care and
   116

care: autoethnographic explorations
   of 15; in community based
   settings 91–92; defined 4; as
   emotional labour 25, 110–113,
   118; medical perspective on
   94–97; nurturing care 128–130;

pastoral care 103–104, 111;
   as reciprocal relation 19–20,
   124; relational approach to 16,
   124–126; as situated act 20, 25,
   127–128; technology and science
   as mechanisms to facilitate care
   62, 68–74; under-theorisation of
   4; as virtue 16; see also autonomy
   and care; caring climate; costs
   of care and commitment; duty of
   care; holistic approach to care;
   self-care
care ceiling 56–57
care ethic see Noddings' care ethic
'care full' and 'care less' workers
   54–55, 56
care paradox 126–127
caring climate 20–24, 25, 88–89,
   95, 127–128
caring for coaches 117–118, 130
caring practice, pedagogical cases
   model for 31
caring relationships: coach-athlete
   relationships as 125–126;
   developing 105, 107–108; as
   dynamic and complex 127;
   see also nurturing relationships
caring school communities 21–22
case study, defined 33
Centre for Safe Sport (US) 3
child protection, work on 3–4
Child Protection in Sport Unit
   (UK) 3

coach-doctor relationships 95–96
coach education programs 88,
    89–90, 92–94, 96–97
coach educators, recommendations
    for 58, 78, 97–98, 119
coach employers, recommendations
    for 58, 118, 119
coaches: caring for 117–118,
    130; duty of care towards
    119; exemplary 16; at medical
    appointments 95; power of 6–7,
    53, 108; as seeking knowledge
    84–86, 87, 88; *see also* 'off the
    field' work of coaches; personal
    lives of coaches
coach researchers, recommendations
    for 58–59, 78, 98, 118–119,
    131–132
collection of pedagogical cases
    37–38
communication in coaching 52–53
community based settings, care in
    91–92
competitive excellence, context
    of 83–84, 92; *see also* winning,
    focus on
competitive world of coaching
    53–57
context of coaching: of Dave
    101–102; of Jane 48–49; of Julie
    83–84; sociology of education
    and 53–57; of Terry 64–66
costs of care and commitment:
    burnout and 113–118; Dave and
    108–109; emotional labour and
    109–113
Cronin, Colum 84, 104
Cronin, Owen 82, 89, 94

data, using to care for athletes
    72–74
deep acting 109–110
dehumanising athletes 70, 74
depersonalisation phase of burnout
    115
development of pedagogical cases
    34–36

dialogue in pedagogical approach
    52–53, 66–67, 75
disadvantaged children, care for
    91–92
display rules 110, 111
duty of care: child protection
    standards and 124; defined 3;
    Jane on 46; relational activity and
    125–126; towards coaches 119;
    of UK coaches 2; work on 3–4

eating habits of athletes 86–87
emotional labour, care as 25,
    110–113, 118
emotion work 109–110, 112
empowerment of athletes 67–68
engrossment 18–19, 25–26, 44, 50, 124
Enright, Kevin 62, 71
exhort feeling 109–110

family life *see* personal lives of
    coaches
feeling rules 110, 111
female athlete triad 86–87, 94–95
first aid, permission to administer 91

Gano-Overway, Lori 24, 89
gender: care ceilings and 56–57;
    care relationships and 17
genuine expression 110–111, 113
Gilligan, Carol 17–18
glass ceiling 47

Hayton, John 103, 109
health, tension between caring
    about performance and caring for
    health 82
Hjälm, Sören 103, 113
Hochschild, Arlie Russell 109–111,
    113
holistic approach to care 97,
    101–102, 107, 108–109

imagine feeling 110
initial phase of burnout 115
injury prevention 84–85
'in loco parentis' 46, 90

in situ based assessment 93
interdisciplinary, physical activity
    as 39
interpersonal relationship, coaching
    as 5–7

kinesiology 10n2
knowledge, coaches as seeking
    84–86, 87, 88

limitations, recognition of 87, 88,
    89, 95, 96
long-term approach to coaching
    65–66, 71, 77
Lynch's sociology of education
    53–57

medical appointments, attendance
    of coaches at 95
medical perspective on care 94–97
modelling caring dispositions 89
motivational displacement 19–20,
    25–26, 44, 50, 124
multidisciplinary climate of care
    88, 95

narratives, case studies as 38–39
national governing body, work with:
    Jane 45, 48, 49; Julie 83; Simon
    92; Terry 63, 65
national team coaching 104–105
National Youth Sport Programme
    (NYSP) 22–23
negative incidents, learning from
    84–85, 87–88
'new managerialism' 53–55, 57
no-compromise approach 54
Noddings' care ethic: autonomy
    and 75; Jane and 45, 49, 50–53;
    limitations of 24–25; overview
    16–20
nurturing care 128–130
nurturing relationships: Jane and
    46, 50–53, 56–58; Terry and 67;
    value of 17, 25
NYSP (National Youth Sport
    Programme) 22–23

'off the field' work of coaches:
    Colum and 44; Dave and
    103–104, 107–108, 111; in
    grassroots football environment
    93; Jane and 50–51; as under
    recognised 129
overtraining 84–85, 86, 87

paradoxical care crisis 2, 126–127
pastoral care 103–104, 111
pedagogical approach, dialogue in
    52–53, 66–67, 75
pedagogical cases: benefits of
    32–33; collection of 37–38;
    Dave 101–103; defined 30, 33;
    development of 34–36; guidelines
    suggested by 130–131; inspiration
    for model for 31–32; Jane
    45–48; Julie 82; model of 30–31;
    overview 125; presentation of
    38–39; relevance of 33–34; Terry
    62–64
pedagogy, defined 33, 50
performance, tension between
    caring for health and caring
    about performance 82
performance domain of sport 65
personal lives of coaches: Dave
    102, 104, 105–107, 112, 118;
    Jane 55, 106; Julie 106
person-centred coaching 105, 107
phenomenological research 34–36,
    124
physical education (PE) teaching
    50, 64
positive youth development through
    basketball 101–102
power of coaches 6–7, 53, 108
presentation of pedagogical cases
    38–39
professional development
    programmes 89–90

reciprocal relation, care as 19–20,
    124
reflection and reorientation for
    burnout 116

reflective practice 87–88
relational approach to care 16,
124–126
Relative Energy Deficiency in Sport
(RED-S) 94–95, 96
remote coaching 48
research: in coaching 5–8;
phenomenological 34–36; to
support practitioners, educators
and employers 131–132;
translational, mechanism for 32
righteous indignation about
unethical coach behaviour 1, 5
rigorous and critical approach to
care 124
Roberts, Simon 82, 89, 92
rule-based relationships 17, 69–70,
77, 129–130

safeguarding, work on 3–4
scaffolding coaching practice 68,
76, 77
scandals of unethical coach
behaviour 1, 5, 126–127
science *see* technology and science,
as mechanisms to facilitate care
self-care 25, 116, 130
situated act, care as 20, 25, 127–128
sleep habits 117
socially vulnerable children, care
for 91–92
sport pedagogy 2–3, 49–50
sports and exercise medicine 94
sport science role in caring for
athletes 62, 71–74, 78

subjective experience and
phenomenological research
34–36

teaching: coaching linked to 2–3,
63–64; feminist perspective on 16;
knowledge required for 33–34;
primary school 46; *see also*
physical education (PE) teaching
Teaching Personal and Social
Responsibility (TPSR) model
22–23
technology and science, as
mechanisms to facilitate care 62,
68–74
tension between caring about
performance and caring for
health 82
training diaries 86
training groups 64–65
translational research, mechanism
for 32

UNICEF 4
United Nations Office on Sport for
Development and Peace 3–4

virtue, care as 16
volunteerism as feature of coaching
49, 65

winning, focus on 82; *see also*
competitive excellence,
context of
women and care ceilings 56–57

Printed in Great Britain
by Amazon

12004339R00088